PRACTICAL MANAGEMENT
PROBLEM SOLVING
AND
DECISION MAKING

PRACTICAL MANAGEMENT
PROBLEM SOLVING
AND
DECISION MAKING

Richard I. Lyles, Ph.D.

 VAN NOSTRAND REINHOLD COMPANY
NEW YORK   CINCINNATI   TORONTO   LONDON   MELBOURNE

Library of Congress Catalog Card Number: 81-19736
ISBN: 0-442-25889-5

Manufactured in the United States of America

Published by Van Nostrand Reinhold Company Inc.
135 West 50th Street, New York, N.Y. 10020

Van Nostrand Reinhold Publishing
1410 Birchmount Road
Scarborough, Ontario MIP 2E7, Canada

Van Nostrand Reinhold Australia Pty. Ltd.
17 Queen Street
Mitcham, Victoria 3132, Australia

Van Nostrand Reinhold Company Limited
Molly Millars Lane
Workingham, Berkshire, England

15   14   13   12   11   10   9   8   7   6   5   4   3   2   1

Library of Congress Cataloging in Publication Data

Lyles, Richard I.
  Practical management problem solving and
decision making.

  Includes index.
  1. Problem solving.   2. Decision-making.
3. Management.   I. Title.
HD30.29.L94   658.4'03   81-19736
ISBN 0-442-25889-5   AACR2

Introduction

It is safe to assume that activity that is organized and carried out in an orderly manner will probably be more efficient and effective over the long run than activity that is not organized. Many good managers and administrators have found this to be especially true with problem-solving and decision-making activity. There seems to be a definite advantage to following a logical sequence of activities and thought processes when attacking a problem or decision. Those who prefer to muddle through appear to have a much more difficult time sustaining high-quality results.

Over the years a number of management experts have proposed different approaches for structuring the activities of problem solving and decision making. Like the evolutionary changes experienced in all aspects of life, our practical knowledge in this area has grown appreciably in the recent past. The more we study, use, and experiment with different approaches, the more we learn. Through this learning greater insights have been developed to help refine your methods to achieve greater efficiency and a higher quality of results.

The book you are about to read is based on an approach I believe is *most practical* in helping managers to achieve the best possible results in the vast majority of problem-solving and decision-making dilemmas they face. To better understand how this approach differs from other approaches, it is important to understand at least two other approaches that have been widely taught and used in the past. These are the Traditional Five-Step approach and the Kepner Tregoe Method.

THE TRADITIONAL FIVE-STEP APPROACH

This approach was the first attempt at organizing the activities associated with solving problems and making decisions. Although there are several variations, the most common form is shown below.

Step 1: Define the Problem
Step 2: Generate Alternatives
Step 3: Select the Best Alternative(s)
Step 4: Implement
Step 5: Monitor the Results

One variation of this method is to insert a data-gathering step between the first two steps. Another variation is to split the third step into two steps—evaluating alternatives and choosing alternatives. In some presentations Step 5 is labeled Evaluate rather than Monitor. In other formats a sixth step is added which is often called "Make necessary corrections." Even though many of these variations actually contain more than five basic steps or sets of activities, they will all be grouped together here for discussion purposes since there are few substantive differences between them.

A prominent characteristic of this approach is that it makes no distinction between decisions and problems. Both decisions and problems are defined generally as "things that need an answer," and this method is taught as a good way to arrive at an answer.

Although still widely used and taught, the strongest criticism of the Five-Step Approach is that it is not structured enough. Critics feel this approach lacks the rigorous thinking and specificity necessary to achieve results with today's management environment. They further state that decisions and problems are different and as such require different approaches and the use of different thought processes to handle them effectively. A final criticism of this approach is that many decisions and solutions to problems fail for reasons unaccounted for in this particular structuring of activities.

In sharp contrast to the Five-Step Approach is the Kepner Tregoe Method.

THE KEPNER TREGOE METHOD

This method was developed after extensive research by Charles Kepner, a social psychologist, and Benjamin Tregoe, a sociologist, who together spent considerable time researching the thought processes people use in the successful resolution of problems and in making decisions. In contrast to the Traditional Five-Step Approach, the Kepner Tregoe Method (or K/T Method, as it is often referred to) is highly rigorous and structured. It is detailed very specifically and treats problem solving and decision making separately.

Kepner and Tregoe employ a seven-step method of Problem Analysis for dealing with problem situations. It is summarized briefly below.

Step 1: Define an expected standard of Performance.
Step 2: Recognize a deviation from the Standard.
Step 3: Precisely Identify, Locate, and Describe the Deviation.
Step 4: Identify the Distinctions and Changes.
Step 5: Find Relevant Changes that are Producing Unwanted Effects.
Step 6: Deduce Possible Causes from the Relevant Changes.
Step 7: Identify the Cause that Exactly Explains all the Facts in the Specification of the Problem.

Problem Analysis would then be followed by Decision Analysis which would be used to determine the best course of action to follow to correct the problem and to restore the operation to productive business activity. Like Problem Analysis, Decision Analysis is comprised of seven steps. They are as follows.

Step 1: Establish the Objectives of the Decision.
Step 2: Classify the Objectives as to Importance.
Step 3: Develop Alternative Actions.
Step 4: Evaluate Alternatives Against Established Objectives.
Step 5: Tentatively Choose the Best Alternative.
Step 6: Explore Tentative Decision for Future Possible Adverse Consequences.
Step 7: Control Effects of the Final Decision by Taking Actions to Prevent Possible Adverse Consequences and by Making Sure Actions Decided on are Carried Out.

In their book, *The Rational Manager* (McGraw-Hill, 1965), Kepner and Tregoe further elaborate on a process called Potential Problem Analysis which also follows a seven-step sequence. The steps of Potential Problem Analysis include:

Step 1: Identify Everything That Could Go Wrong.
Step 2: Describe in Detail Each Potential Problem.
Step 3: Prioritize the Potential Problems According to Risk.
Step 4: List All Possible Causes for Each Potential Problem.
Step 5: Rate the Probability Each Cause is Likely to Occur.
Step 6: Identify Preventative Actions.
Step 7: Prepare to Take Contingency Actions in Case the Problem Cannot be Prevented.

The Kepner Tregoe approach relies heavily on an individual manager learning how to structure his/her thought processes. A fairly rigorous attention to detail is necessary in order to achieve success. Although the K/T approach is thorough, it has received criticism from those who have learned to use it.

The major criticism of the Kepner Tregoe Method is that it is too cumbersome for the vast majority of problems and decisions most managers routinely encounter. Problem Analysis relies on either a historical or a comparative data base for successful application. Without these data (which many problems lack) it is impossible to identify distinctions and isolate causes using the K/T method. K/T Decision Analysis is most useful when a finite number of alternatives is readily identifiable, but is often criticized for being of little help in developing creative solutions to complex problems. K/T methods lean heavily on rigid and "rational" thought processes, leaving little room for flexibility or judgmental factors. Because of the jargon used in teaching the process, those who have become skilled in the K/T approach frequently encounter difficulty in communicating with those who have not had the same training. Thus, the K/T processes seem to work best in highly technical situations and have proven to be least helpful in dealing with the more ambiguous human and operational situations most managers encounter more frequently. And finally, K/T relies heavily on the premise that there is always one and only one "best and right answer," and all one needs to do is to find this singularly unique solution and everything wil fall into place naturally.

THE LYLES METHOD

The book you are about to read is based on an approach developed by me during the course of my work as a manager and a management consultant for the past ten years. It differs from the Five-Step and Kepner Tregoe approaches in several ways. The Lyles Method places strong emphasis on flexibility and on achieving optimum results with a variety of problem types under varying conditions, without being cumbersome. Emphasis is placed on reducing or eliminating unnecessary activity to avoid trading bottom-line performance for skillfully carried out activity.

The Lyles Method consists of six steps when applied to decision making and seven steps when applied to problem solving. It includes specific steps directed toward communicating and troubleshooting, recognizing that both are critical for achieving final success. The method is illustrated below.

THE LYLES METHOD

When problems are encountered all seven steps would be employed, as indicated by the arrows on the right. Only the last six steps would be used in decision-making situations. An underlying premise of this method is that decision-making and problem-solving activities do *not* occur in isolation as individual events. As Joseph Cooper said in *The Art of Decision Making* (Doubleday, 1961),

A single decision is merely a moment in time. Once it is made and carried into effect, it precipitates changes in the environment of the decision. Then new problems are created for which new solutions are required. Hence, if you think you have settled things and that you can relax for a while, you are deceiving yourself. The ever-present forces of change compel an endless updating of decisions and actions. New conditions, new experiences and new information are always coming up to require the modification of goals, policies, programs or procedures and the creation of new ones.

The problem-solving and decision-making techniques presented in this book take into account the reality that managers operate in a dynamic and changing world. Deciding what outcomes to pursue is the first decision of management. Thus defining objectives (specifying end-result outcomes) is the starting point for organized management activity. When problems arise they cause new information to rise to the surface. New information drives new decisions. Although there is a sequential process that allows these forces to be dealt with systematically, it is important to remember that the overall situation is dynamic and ever-changing. This requires on-line flexibility on the part of the manager.

Practical Management Problem Solving presents different strategies to use in different kinds of situations to optimize your performance as a problem solver and decision maker. My experience has been that there are three natural categories these situations can be divided into, and that decisions and problems arising in each category deserve different treatment because of the dynamics they are likely to create. The three categories of problems and decisions are people, operating, and technical. All the concepts, skills, and strategies are thus presented to provide as much flexibility as possible in solving different types of problems and making decisions in these different areas.

Special thanks and acknowledgment go to M. Wayne Wilson, Ph.D., whose ideas, creative insights, suggestions, and help contributed substantially to the formation of the contents of the book and the ideas presented. Wayne's insatiable curiosity and unending creativity inspired me immeasurably to write this book. Now I know why so many authors extend their appreciation to their spouse upon completion of a book. It is not merely a matter of courtesy. My wife Martha contributed a great deal to the book through her creative insights, helpful suggestions, proofreading, and most of all support and encouragement when the pressure was on to meet deadlines. I must also thank my parents for their support, and especially my father, who was more than willing to bounce his management wisdom off my ideas and strengthen my thinking.

Richard I. Lyles, Ph.D.

Contents

INTRODUCTION / v

PART I.   Foundations for Problem Solving and Decision Making / 1

1. Understanding Decision-Making and Problem-Solving Activity / 3
2. Factors to Consider When Solving Problems and Making Decisions / 24
3. Overall Strategy / 42

PART II.   Seven Steps to Practical Problem Solving and Decision Making for Managers / 69

4. Defining the Problem / 71
5. Defining Objectives / 89
6. Generating Alternatives / 105
7. Developing Action Plans / 124
8. Troubleshooting / 150
9. Communicating / 166
10. Implementing / 183

Index / 197

PRACTICAL MANAGEMENT
PROBLEM SOLVING
AND
DECISION MAKING

Part I
Foundations for
Problem Solving and
Decision Making

1
Understanding Decision–Making and Problem–Solving Activity

Before discussing the specific activities of problem solving and decision making, an observation regarding management in general is in order. The observation relates to the importance of mission, goals, and objectives to effective management. These are the keystones to sound management, for they form the criteria and base of reference for all other management activity. If a manager has a cloudy, vague, and ambiguous sense of personal and organizational purpose, that manager's results will be equally nebulous. On the other hand, the manager with a clear and crisp sense of purpose will produce noticeable results.

There is a hierarchy of purpose, with each level making its special contribution to overall performance. First comes *mission,* which is the organization's overall purpose or long-range reason for being. Next are *goals,* which are short- and long-range major accomplishments leading to the fulfillment of the mission. *Objectives* are next—they are the measurable steps leading to the achievement of goals. And finally, *action plans* and *schedules* become the detailed maps which lay out a specific sequence of events and activities to be performed by the members of the organization. Although these terms may have slightly different meanings in different organizations, these definitions are most common, and as such will be used in this book.

A clearly thought-through hierarchy of purpose and intended results does not guarantee effective organization performance or good management. However, it is a necessary condition to achieve sustained positive results. Organizations can only be successful if there is a reasonably accurate understanding throughout the organization of its purpose and desired results. This holds true whether the organization is a work group of six or less, a section, a department, a division, a group, a company, or a multinational corporation.

Objectives change over time, varying from situation to situation. Although major goals and purpose are less likely to change in any substantive way over the short run, objectives may vary in accordance with the need to overcome the numerous operational problems and obstacles likely to be encountered in daily operations. Thus it is an important process of all decision-making and problem-solving activities to define specific desired outcomes for each decision or problem solution. New situations cause new information to surface, and new information drives new decisions. It is thus necessary to rethink objectives, eliminating the obsolete and adding the new, to keep abreast of events, and waste as little effort as possible on nonproductive activity.

> Responsible management action is guided by clear-cut objectives. Good managers will continually ask, "WHAT DO WE WANT TO ACHIEVE?"

More will be said about this in Chapter 5, but is worth noting here that objectives should be considered on several different levels. Most decision-making and problem-solving processes limit this activity, when used, to defining the specific objectives of the individual decision or problem under consideration. However, by defining the context of ACHIEVE, the Lyles Method attempts to force a linkage between short-range activities and overall management results.

IDENTIFYING DIFFERENT ALTERNATIVES

Although it is important to have clearly defined objectives, it is not enough. It is imperative that managers recognize there are many different paths that can eventually lead to the achievement of a given set of objectives. In identifying different courses of action, the manager should always remember that no two sets of circumstances are the same. Although a similar situation may have been encountered earlier with similar objectives defined, it is possible the two situations could demand markedly different responses. Therefore, in any given circumstance, it is important to identify all possible courses of action to achieve the desired results. Although it is not common, managers occasionally find the best course of action in a current situation to be an alternative that was rejected earlier in what appeared to be a similar set of circumstances.

In addition to considering alternatives when problems arise or objectives are refined, managers should also develop the habit of considering alternative courses of action when things are going well. This kind of concurrent critiquing can contribute greatly to productivity and efficiency gains. It can also foster the overall process of critical thinking, so when problems and decision dilemmas arise, the manager is better prepared to perform.

> Another key for the focus of management activity then, is "WHAT ALTERNATIVES EXIST?"

CHOOSING A COURSE OF ACTION

Having identified different courses of action for consideration, it then becomes necessary to decide which course of action to pursue. Rarely, if ever, is an organization or manager confronted with only one set of potential outcomes or a single approach to achieve those outcomes. Usually there are several alternatives to choose from and more often than not, the choices do not lend themselves to simple comparison. Consider, for example, the following:

- A marketing manager confronted with a decision to expand the share in a declining market or drop the product and go into new product lines.

- The research and development manager who must decide whether to spend limited capital on short-range, moderate-risk, moderate-payoff projects, or to invest in longer range, higher risk, higher payoff projects.

- The quality assurance supervisor in a reasonably reliable production line who can reduce the tests and meet the shipping dates on a rush order, or rigidly insist on completing all tests to ensure quality, but miss the shipping date.

In each of these cases, the manager has to make a decision—to judge different sets of alternatives (and their perceived consequences). It's worth noting that this rarely represents a choice between "right" and "wrong." Management choices are rarely that absolute. Usually each alternative will have advantages and disadvantages, and both positive and negative potential consequences which all must be weighed, so when the final judgment is rendered, the chosen course of action will bring the organization closest to its intended position.

> Managers must make choices between alternate courses of action, waiting until all possible consequences have been considered to ask, "WHAT SHOULD WE DO?"

PREVENTING FUTURE PROBLEMS

Having definite objectives and a specific course of action to pursue is still not enough to produce optimum results. Others in the organization will be working toward their objectives, and some conflict is inevitable. Circumstances in existence today will change tomorrow. New needs will arise and priorities will shift. To assume that a course of action chosen today will survive unscathed tomorrow is naive at best. Therefore, it is important to try to determine as best as possible what is likely to go wrong.

Problem solving in advance is one of the most efficient kinds of problem solving a manager can accomplish. Anticipatory thinking skills are among the most valuable tools a manager can have available. These will enable the development of *preventive action* steps to take to avoid possible problems, or *contingency actions* to take if the problem situations should arise. In either case, if these actions are considered in advance and anticipated, the results should be far better than if they are developed on the spur of the moment in a "crisis management" mode.

> Valuable gains can be achieved by devoting time to determining possible problems in advance—by asking, "WHAT MIGHT GO WRONG?"

COMMMUNICATING FOR RESULTS

The best laid action plans often fail because of confusion in implementation or lack of understanding and support. Top-quality plans always contain a plan to communicate the plan. Everyone who will be affected (either positively or negatively) by the actions should be notified prior to implementation of the plan. First they should be made aware of your predicament and objectives. Then they should be given enough information so they can understand how to act responsibly. People don't do dumb things deliberately—rather they act on the information that is available to them. If you are the manager responsible for achieving your objectives, then you also have the responsibility to ensure those who can have an effect on your results have the necessary information so they can act positively, or at the very least, get out of the way.

Far too many plans fail because someone didn't get the word. You can avoid this by taking that extra bit of time up front to ensure the right messages get to the proper place. Failure to do so will mean taking the short cut that turns out to be the long cut in the long run.

> "WHAT SHOULD OTHERS KNOW?" is the question to ask to make sure you elicit the proper support from those upon whom your success depends.

IMPLEMENTATION

Once a course of action has been chosen and the direction set and communicated, implementation activities become an ongoing challenge. The first step is to identify and specify individuals to be held accountable for the accomplishment of the objectives. In each case, accountability for the final consequences should rest with a single person. Dual accountability or joint accountability rarely works satisfactorily. For each intended result, only one person should be given responsibility.

The next step is to ensure all directions and intended actions have been communicated accurately—close the feedback loop by asking people *what* they understood (not *if* they understood).

Then establish standards and reporting procedures. These should be defined with sufficient specificity so management can readily compare actual progress to the plan. They should also be cost effective. In other words, the information produced should not cost more than it is worth.

Specific schedules for reporting measurements of progress toward goals should be developed next. These reporting schedules should be established based on the assumption that things will go as planned. Another way of saying this is to say that wise managers plan for competency and accomplishment rather than incompetence and failure.

Recognizing that problems are inevitable, however, good managers will also incorporate warning systems into their activities to warn as early as possible of impending trouble. No matter how well the trouble-shooting was carried out, certain unpredictable problems and phenomena will still occur. Because of the inevitability of problems and unforeseen circumstances, it is also worth noting that individual managers or employees should not feel guilty when circumstances require them to take corrective action. This should be seen as a normal and predictable kind of management activity.

> Good management requires good tracking skills aimed at finding out, "WHAT'S HAPPENING?"

PROBLEM SOLVING

Again, it is inevitable that obstacles and problems will arise that will block the path toward organizational achievement. It is doubtful an organization will achieve anything of substance without encountering problems in the process. However, this is not necessarily bad.

Contrary to popular assumption, problems can provide several valuable benefits. First of all, they challenge the thought processes and force creative thinking. Second, they encourage situations to be examined from different perspectives, frequently causing new and better methods to be employed. Third, they usually act as a catalyst for personal learning among the people involved. And finally, problem situations quite often carry with them the seeds for new opportunities.

The message here is not that each manager should immediately go forth and try to create problems in order to reap these benefits. Nor should good managers sit idly by, eagerly awaiting the next problem to surface. However, it is important to recognize that in any organizational effort of meaningful significance, problems are unavoidable. In fact, the presence of problems from time to time is probably one valid indicator that the organization is producing meaningful results.

There's an old story about two managers discussing the performance of a third associate. One commented about how much he envied the third manager because he has worked for the past year without encountering a single problem. "Yes," replied the second manager, "but he hasn't produced a single result, either." It is easy to avoid problems by doing nothing.

When problems arise, the first course of action is to define the problem. In other words, one must first determine what is wrong. This means identifying and describing the obstacles, conditions, or phenomena which now stand in the way of achieving objectives or are causing a deviation from the desired status. In essence, the outcome of this activity is new information about current situation and circumstances. Once this is understood, activity should then shift to the next step, define objectives. Don't worry about "solving the problem" until objectives have been reviewed and evaluated in light of the new situation. The cause of the problem may or may not be worth worrying about, depending on future objectives.

> Finding out the answer to the question, "WHAT IS WRONG?" is important, but it should be asked in the context of overall objectives, responsibilities, and priorities.

OVERALL APPROACH AND CONTEXT

Integrated into a total scheme then, problem-solving and decision-making activity can be presented as follows:

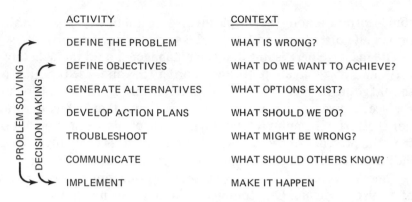

CONTEXT FOR PROBLEM—SOLVING AND
DECISION—MAKING ACTIVITY
THE LYLES METHOD

To help focus on the appropriate context during each phase of activity a more detailed definition of the different activities might be helpful. The following listing of activities includes brief, but more descriptive definitions of each.

Define the Problem	Identify and describe obstacles, conditions, or phenomena which stand in the way of achieving objectives or are causing a deviation from the desired status.
Define Objectives	Delineate and describe specific, end-result outcomes to be achieved. The definition of objectives should address the short-term purpose of the immediate issues being addressed as well as the long-range goals of management.
Generate Alternatives	Develop a broad range of possible actions to take to achieve the specified objectives.
Develop Action Plans	Determine the most efficient course of action to achieve the specified objective(s).
Troubleshoot	Predict problems that are likely to occur when action is taken and identify avoidance and reactive actions to minimize the effects of these potential problems.

Communicate	Inform those affected of your intentions and expectations so they understand and will support you in achieving your objectives.
Implement	Initiate action to achieve the specified objectives and sustain the desired consequences.

DIFFERENT KINDS OF PROBLEMS

With the exception of certain kinds of mechanical failure or equipment breakdown, no two problems are the same. Rarely, if ever, is a manager likely to encounter two decisions or two problems that are identical. Contrary to the popular myth, history never repeats itself exactly.

However, there are different categories of problems with characteristic similarities. An understanding of these categories, and the commonalities of the problems within each category, can be of great benefit to a manager. The three basic categories of problems are:

1. People—problems caused primarily by the behavior of an individual or group of people.
2. Operational—problems caused primarily by factors other than people or technology. These include such things as policy, organization structure, dynamics of the marketplace or the economy, and problems stemming from laws and regulations. Problems in the functional specialties of finance, marketing, operations, public relations, communications, planning, and evaluation would all fall in this area.
3. Technical—problems caused primarily by mechanical, technical, electrical, electronic, or hydraulic equipment component, and/or system functioning or failure to function.

In discussing the different types of problems and the different factors which cause individual problems to be assigned to different categories, it is important to understand the various levels on which analysis can be conducted, and to remember that here we are looking at the level of primary cause.

For every outcome or consequence an organization produces there is a basic and fundamental cause. This fundamental level is referred to as the causal level. It is becoming more common for managers, particularly when problem solving, to say they are looking for causality. This means they are looking for the primary root-cause of a particular effect or set of outcomes. Causal level events are the triggering events. They are the events, conditions, or phenomena that start the chain reactions which ultimately create a desired or undesired effect.

The next level of variables are referred to as either shaping variables or intervening variables. These are the things that occur at the intermediate points in the chain reaction which alter or shape the final effects or outcomes. These are events, conditions, or phenomena that would likely not matter were it not for the causal events of a particular situation, but given those circumstances generally have a definite effect on final impact.

The final level is the output level. These are data or conditions of final effect. Analysis conducted at this level is end-results analysis, taking into account that this is the end of the chain. Attempts to solve problems by addressing concerns or variables at this level amounts to little more than window dressing and usually just barely penetrates beneath the surface.

Thus it is important when making decisions or solving problems that the manager know what level—either causal, intervening, or output—variable is being addressed. Much time can be saved and stronger results achieved if issues are addressed and decided on the appropriate level. The difference one might achieve by examining a problem on different levels can best be demonstrated with an example. A particularly good example for this purpose might be the nuclear reactor breakdown at the nuclear power-generating plant at Three Mile Island.

In very simple terms, the following occurred at Three Mile Island. A valve malfunctioned, causing the system to go awry. In response to the valve malfunctioning, operators made at least one error in judgment, causing things to get worse. The end result is a dome full of poisonous gas that will take years to dispose of.

With these facts as a basis, then, the problem at Three Mile Island would fall under the category of being a technical problem. The primary cause of the entire chain of events was a malfunctioning valve. Problems are categorized based on their causality. Even though the problem was greatly affected by events at the intervening or shaping level by the actions and inactions of various people, the problem is really a technical problem. There is no doubt that what happened at the intervening level had a direct and substantial effect on the final result. Had the proper course of action been taken the results could very likely have been a limited period of time during which the reactor would be shut down and then things would have been back to normal. As it is now, if one were only to examine the existing set of circumstances, it might be easy to draw the conclusion that the only problem to confront is more of an operational problem. That is, how to get rid of the poisonous gas and get back to work.

It is easy to see now that addressing the problem on either the output level or the intervening level will be insufficient to completely prevent similar kinds of problems in the future. Although the gas must be disposed of, doing so won't eliminate the danger of similar accidents occurring elsewhere. Training operators to respond properly when malfunctions occur is justified and appropriate. However, the potential for future problems of a similar nature will never be eliminated until the malfunctioning valve is either replaced, improved, or provided with a backup. Until causality has been dealt with directly, the problem cannot be considered solved.

With this analytical framework in mind, consider the following problems and more detailed descriptions of the three different categories of problems.

PEOPLE PROBLEMS

This category includes all the problems of management that at the causal level are triggered primarily by human behavior. In other words, the source of the problem is a person or group of people. These are problems in which the solutions will be arrived at by causing behavior changes. Consider the following cases, all presented exactly as submitted by the managers who encountered them.

People Problem A

Harold Sampson has been employed by Wacket Manufacturing Company for five years during which time he has always filled the same position, doing the same job. He is considered to be an expert in his product line and is the only person left in the department who can handle the remaining product in the line. This product is expected to be phased out in about one year. His attendance and quality of work have been acceptable.

The problem is Harold's excessive use of company telephones for personal business without getting prior permission from his supervisor. Harold is a union employee. He has had two verbal warnings and two written reprimands issued in the presence of a union steward (who agreed that the reprimands were appropriate). The company is faced with an exceptionally heavy workload, a replacement for Harold would require six months of training to obtain anything close to the level of expertise Harold currently maintains, and the product is likely to be gone within a year, anyway. What can be done?

People Problem B

Sandy is a supervisor in a busy office. Her immediate boss is Jerry. Jerry is a knowledgeable and efficient manager. He has a record of good employee relations, as well as improving office equipment and methods. Sandy has a reputation within her office of being an organized and efficient supervisor. Sandy and Jerry are both pleasant people and are generally liked by those they service as well as the inner office staff.

Of late, Sandy has started to feel a wall of resistance building between her and Jerry. This is bothering her for several reasons: (1) She and Jerry are both very progressive and productive. She believes they make a good team and doesn't want it to deteriorate. (2) Sandy has noticed that Jerry appears agitated when she questions schedules, delayed supplies, *etc.* Recently, Sandy asked Jerry for some private time so they could discuss many items regarding inner office needs and pending schedules. Jerry was agreeable and told Sandy that he would possibly have time tomorrow. The next day Sandy was put off due to his heavy work schedule. Due to other commitments, Sandy and Jerry both knew it might be a week before they could have the needed meeting, so Sandy was upset when she later saw Jerry spend the afternoon in his office in an obviously relaxed, nonworking "bull" session.

People Problem C

Borgen Manufacturing operated a second shift with twelve people. The first line supervisor from the day shift left the company and the second shift supervisor was transferred to the vacated position, leaving the supervisory position for the second shift open. In the period prior to the position being filled, numerous rumors circulated regarding who might be selected to fill the position. There were also rumors that if certain people, and one person in particular was given the job, about half the people on the shift would quit the company.

One evening the transferring supervisor called a meeting of all second shift personnel to discuss the selection of his replacement. For no apparent reason, a physical fight broke out between two of the people. Upon further inquiry into the matter, the supervisor found out the following. Within the group of second shift employees, three cliques had formed, each social subgroup comprised of four people. One of the groups was made up of individuals who were all gay, and in the past few weeks they had become increasingly more open about their homosexuality and were threatening the others that they were going to "take over the second shift." Although everyone on the shift had been performing satisfactorily without major problems in the past, the tension between the three factions had increased dramatically during just the past few weeks.

People Problem D

Two service groups of a large bank work in close proximity providing a service used by a third group. Both of the service groups have suffered losses in senior personnel resulting in lower productivity within the groups, and tension and unhealthy competition between the two groups. Members from neither group appreciate the difficulties the other group has in providing the needed services. Nor do they understand that total efficiency for the entire bank depends upon them working together supportively and in harmony rather than the way they are currently working. The problem is gradually getting worse as each group is becoming more and more self-centered and hostile toward the other.

Although each of these four cases describe people problems, the incidents require analytical approaches on four separate levels. Problem A, Harold Sampson losing interest in his work, describes a people problem that is occurring at the *intrapersonal* level. Problem B, the breakdown in communications between Sandy and Jerry, is an *interpersonal* problem. The group of second shift workers struggling for control of supervision, which is Problem C, is a problem of *intragroup* conflict. And Problem D, two service groups on a collision course, is a problem of *intergroup* functioning. See Chapter 4 for a more detailed presentation of the levels and the use of these concepts in defining different kinds of problems.

An important point regarding people problems is that although the main concern with this type problem is human behavior, the best course of action to resolve the problem frequently does *not* include either direct manipulation or confrontation of the behavior in question. The solutions that often work best are solutions that cause the desired change through indirect means rather than face-to-face confrontation. The following case demonstrates the point.

The General Services Department of a fairly large city's organization is responsible for trash collection throughout the city. Jack Watson supervises six of the trash collection crews in the solid waste disposal division. Several months ago Jack began receiving complaints about one of his crew's performance. Citizens complained that the crew would empty their trash cans by banging them furiously on the side gate of the truck and would then throw the cans back toward the sidewalk. The result was badly dented cans with limited future use and a street that looked like a tornado had been through and scattered cans everywhere.

Jack had numerous talks with his crew to no avail. They said that neighborhood kids on bikes had a favorite game of riding down the street after the crew and competing with each other to see how far they could kick the neatly lined up empty cans without falling off their bikes. According to the crew this is what accounted for the dented and scattered cans. Although Jack doubted their story, there was little he felt he could do. Following the crew to catch them in the act was not practical. Nor was rotating the routes among different crews. Jack had discussed the problem wtih his boss and other crews without success. Nobody could come up with a workable solution.

The problem here is obvious: A trash collection crew is damaging and scattering cans. The objective is also obvious: Get them to do the job right. This is clearly a people problem because it is being caused by the unacceptable behavior of the crew and the solution depends on achieving a desired level of performance. The challenge lies in determining an effective way to do this.

Let's go back to a point made previously. The best course of action in some cases is not necessarily a course of action that will focus directly on the behavior itself. This is especially true in this case. Because of the geographical separation between Jack and his crew, Jack is not in a good position to directly influence the crew's job in the field. Although he may be successful with other crews, his direct confrontations with this crew, no matter how assertive or skilled, are unlikely to produce results any better than those he has already achieved. Without absolute proof, which would be time consuming and almost impossible to obtain, firing the crew would be impractical, since the action would probably be overturned by the Civil Service Commission on appeal. But there is an answer.

In order to understand the solution to this problem and why it worked, some knowledge of the division's operating procedures is necessary. Each morning every member of the division reports to work at 7:00 A.M. After a short stand-up briefing by the supervisor, the crews board their trucks and begin collecting trash. Each route consists of slightly less than a full day's workload, accounting for transit time to the dump, clean-up time, and other routine matters. Existing policy allows for crews who finish early to clock out when they have completed their work and still receive a full day's pay, assuming there is no additional work to be done because of excessive truck breakdowns on other routes, *etc*. Sometimes overtime is required, in which case the crews receive overtime pay for staying late. Although the workers have to stay the full eight hours occasionally, and less frequently they have to work overtime, they most often get off about a half-hour early and receive the full day's pay.

When asked how he had confronted the poorly performing crew previously, Jack said he always talked to them about the problem during the morning stand-up sessions. Jack realized this probably wasn't the most effective approach because of the snickers and whispered remarks he heard from other workers when the subject was discussed. He was reluctant to spend the time a more private conversation would require until the thought was suggested to schedule the meeting at a different time. A few days later the complaints started pouring in again and Jack implemented his plan. It was a Friday and Jack received a dozen calls. That afternoon the crew returned to the yard forty-five minutes before quitting time, racing to clock out and go off to enjoy the weekend. Jack stopped them and expressed his concern about the problem. He said he understood about the kids on the bikes, but since all this was having an effect on the division's image in the community, he felt it was their responsibility to at least try to solve it. Since no one else was around and they had a sizable chunk of time left in the day, he told them he thought this would be an excellent time to attack the problem. Although Jack and the crew never finally arrived at a solution for preventing the kids from kicking over the cans, after two of these "after work" problem-solving sessions, the problem mysteriously disappeared.

OPERATIONAL PROBLEMS

Operational problems differ from people problems in that they are usually more tangible, making it easier for the problem solver to isolate and analyze the variables in the problem. Where human behavior often seems vague and the causes ambiguous, the substance of operational problems is usually much more concrete. Operational problems are problems of organization, policy, market competition, regulation, control, production, accounting, finance, and administration. They are not by nature more or less challenging, nor are they by nature more or less important, than people problems. But they are different. Consider the following examples.

Operational Problem A

Top management in the division of a major electronics manufacturer formed an Inventory Task Force to study current procedures, identify weaknesses, and recommend improvements. Each major department manager commited several people from his/her department to participate in the effort. The task force was divided into teams and assigned a variety of subject areas to study. Each team had a leader. Objectives, tasks, and expected output were specified for each team. The project was urgent, with very short times allowed. Specific target dates in the near future were imposed by top management. As a result, many members were committed by their department managers to full- or half-time work on the project.

As the task-force teams started to work on their assignments, it became immediately evident that the verbal commitments made with regard to the availability of people would not be honored. One individual who had been committed to the task force for full-time work was sent out of town the next day. Others were given priorities by their managers precluding work on the task force.

Operational Problem B

Elegant Engineering and Manufacturing Company has always operated in the past with a philosophy and policy of accepting development orders for custom parts only if there was an accompanying order for follow-on production sales. Examination of this practice led to the discovery that the company was suffering significant losses on production orders that were priced and accepted prior to the development of the part. Because it was almost impossible to accurately predict yield, unexpected production problems, and other cost factors, the company decided to change its policy. A new policy was issued stating that no fixed price production orders were to be accepted starting immediately until after completion of the development of a working part under the development order and all actual costs are known.

In the short time preceding the issuance of the new policy a number of quotes were given to customers for both development and fixed price production orders. The way the policy is worded, these production orders cannot be honored. However, to back out on them would not only upset the customers, it could also possibly generate legal problems. A number of other good customers have stated that if Elegant Engineering can't cost both kinds of orders simultaneously, they will take their business to another company.

Operational Problem C

Cringle Chemical Company is a growing and reasonably profitable supplier of chemical products. The Board of Directors has authorized management to introduce one new product this year. Management has narrowed the possible alternatives down to two. Each of the two products would be introduced into different markets and both have advantages and disadvantages.

Product One has a distinct advantage over anything in its market and represents a significant technical breakthrough. However, the market is pretty well satisfied with present products and shows a 94% customer satisfaction. The total market is about $11.2 million with one strongly entrenched company. This market is stable, but would be a new one for Cringle—their marketing force knows little about the industry. The laboratory group has extremely high confidence in the product and claims it has a clear superiority over the other products on the market. A few Cringle executives think Cringle could benefit by diversifying into a new and different market.

Product Two would be introduced into a market in which Cringle has a good reputation. The product isn't really as good as existing products, but is in a class of products that the market seems to be shifting steadily toward. Cringle has the best product, but the market is shifting away from their product toward the other class which now has 62% of sales. This is a tricky field. Everyone in the market is always trying something new. The market has three strong competitors, and about five selling off brands for a total market of $40 million. Sales in this areas last year accounted for 26% of Cringle's sales, although sales in this area were down 10% for Cringle while the total market grew. Some executives feel Cringle should concentrate on their areas of greatest strength and introduce Product Two.

These three cases demonstrate the diversity in content to be experienced in operational problem solving. Problem A could easily be mistaken for a people problem because the symptoms relate to people not performing as they should. The important distinction here, however, is that anyone in the same set of circumstances would probably have responded in the same way. The problem, when examined at the causal or root level, is really one of organization. A special organizational group was formed without adequate structure in the form of accountability, responsibility, and reporting lines of authority. Good organization doesn't just happen. It is the result of good planning and consideration of the realities of ongoing pressures. Problem B is more obviously an operational problem, dealing with a policy change directly conflicting with previously established practice and the desires of the customer. Problem C is typical of the ever-present decisions management must make regarding the pursuit of future business goals.

TECHNICAL PROBLEMS

Although many technical problems are extremely difficult and challenging to solve, the category of technical problems is probably the easiest to understand. These are problems caused by mechanical, electrical, electronic, hydraulic, component, and/or system malfunctioning. As dealt with here, the emphasis is not on developing technical or scientific solutions to problems of engineering and science. Rather it is on managerial problem solving and decision approaches to responsibly carrying out the necessary actions required to fulfill management responsibilities that are adversely affected when this kind of problem arises. Consider the following problem.

Technical Problem A

A medium-sized plastics company manufactures a special foam laminate product that is blown thin and attached to carpet padding to allow the padding to slide easily during installation. It is their newest and most profitable product. An exceptionally large number of sample runs were conducted and all met with extreme customer satisfaction. Two weeks ago the company went into full production and 30% of the carpeting is failing to laminate to the foam padding properly. It just doesn't stick. The problem isn't localized to just a few customers, but seems to be pretty well generalized. Sample runs are still being run and they continue to be 100% problem free.

This problem has a lot in common with the kind of technical problems managers typically confront. Something is obviously going wrong somewhere in the production process or 30% of the product would not be going bad. However, not enough is known to be able to simply go to an engineer or some other person with technical expertise and tell them to solve it. The cause or causes must first be isolated and then a determination can be made as to whether the solution lies in developing a technically oriented answer or in changing some aspect of the process. The case above was finally solved by a manager, not a technical expert.

Another important consideration in dealing with technical problems is sensitivity about technological systems functioning as a whole. Failure to account for idiosyncrancies that arise when components are tested individually then combined to perform as a system can lead to grave consequences. This is precisely what occurred in two early crashes of the DC-10. Designers didn't realize that accidental decompression of the cargo compartment would ruin several critical parts of the plane's control system.

WHERE FROM HERE?

One thing for certain in management is that we will never have a short-age of either problems or decisions. There is no way to avoid them. To attempt to do so would be suicidal. It is therefore essential that, as managers, we aggressively confront and resolve them in the best possi-ble way, taking into account both similarities and differences to attain the highest level of results. Successful application of the Lyles Method to achieve high-quality results depends on the extent to which an in-dividual manager adopts three distinct principles.

The first principle is mastery of the method and rigorous adherence to the approach. The seven phases of the Lyles Method should be con-sciously followed and adhered to in all cases, recognizing that in cer-tain circumstances one or more phase of activity may receive only cur-sory attention and limited time. It is not important that a large amount of time be spent on each phase of activity in every case. Time spent does not correlate with importance. It is only important that each activity receive attention, even though the attention may be nothing more than deciding on a fast and cursory strategy for a given phase in a particular situation.

The second principle is that there are certain background factors that will inevitably affect the manager's results. Many of these factors are such that they cannot be addressed formally with any kind of pro-cedure or structured format or formula. Where people are involved (and all management activity has a social dimension) there will always

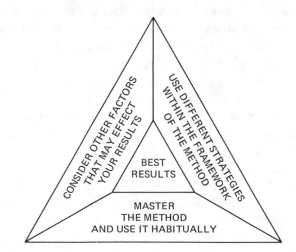

be certain factors that will affect the results, yet are too abstract to quantify. However, these factors need to be taken into account on the highest possible level of conscious awareness. A number of these factors are discussed in detail in Chapter 2.

The final principle in the use of different strategies to apply the method in different situations. The method is the same in all cases, but the strategies will vary depending on the needs at hand. Chapter 3 presents a number of overall strategy considerations along with guidelines for making appropriate strategy selections. Chapters 4 through 10 give several strategies for each of the seven steps in the process.

2
Factors to Consider When
Solving Problems and Making Decisions

For years the debate has raged concerning whether management is an art or a science. Without taking sides or further confusing the issue, let us at least agree that it is a practice. The practice of management depends on a variety of factors that contribute to or detract from the quality of each manager's final results. Although these factors are of such a nature that it is not feasible to address them formally when we structure specific management activity, it is imperative that they be recognized and taken into account when taking management action.

This chapter presents a number of factors that frequently make a difference in the results managers are likely to realize when solving problems and making decisions. They are presented at this time for a reason. These issues are always in the background. It is important then, that before getting into a detailed analysis of all the phases of problem-solving and decision-making activity that we properly set the stage. Without the background firmly established, all activity that takes place in the forefront will have considerably less value. Here then, are number of factors operating in the background and affecting the results of problem-solving and decision-making efforts. They are presented in no particular order because all are important. The relative importance of each in any given situation will vary with the circumstances. The exception to this rule is the results factor. Results will always be the most important and ever-present consideration regardless of circumstance.

CAMELS ARE OKAY

A long-standing joke among managers presents an interesting definition for the word camel. Simply stated, it says a camel is a horse put together by a committee. An underlying message then, is that camels are inferior to horses and should be avoided if possible. Just the opposite is true. To achieve success in organizations of any size requires a certain amount of "camel-building" skill. The following example illustrates the point.

Marvin Wilson is one of twenty work group supervisors who reports to one of four department heads in a product line of a medium-sized manufacturing firm with three product lines. Marvin has been frustrated because he has repeatedly made suggestions for improvements and has received little or no response from higher levels of management. He has good ideas to help achieve his objectives but nobody seems to listen or care. Although it may be easy to place the blame on upper management, the problem is Marvin's and he is in the best position to solve it.

Before discussing how best to solve it however, let's look at Marvin's situation from a broader view point. It's safe to assume Marvin isn't the only supervisor with good ideas and objectives he's eager to accomplish. Most supervisors have at least one good idea and several key objectives at any given time. Multiply this by Marvin's twenty peer-level supervisors then multiply that result by four to take into consideration each department. Then multiply again by three for each product line. The result is a huge number of ideas and objectives being pushed by a large number of individuals, all at once. All these people have their "special horse" they're trying to groom and race across the finish line in first place—in all, a lot of competition. To ensure his horse gets across the finish line, Marvin has to build a camel. Here's how he does it.

Let's call Marvin's horse (his pet idea) AB, and assume that in order to implement AB he must gain approval from the two levels immediately above him in the organization.

The first thing Marvin should do is identify his immediate supervisor's most pressing concerns. Then he must identify the most important priorities of his supervisor's boss. It is imperative Marvin do this investigation thoroughly enough so he knows for sure their important concerns and objectives. Having done this, Marvin then builds a camel—he takes it upon himself to integrate.

Let's call the immediate supervisor's priorities CD. The second supervisor's concerns we'll call EF. After studying the situation, Marvin builds a camel (proposal) that looks like this:

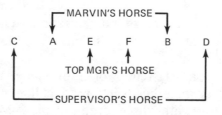

FIGURE 2-1. How to Build a Camel.

Next Marvin takes the time to prepare a formal proposal to communicate the value of doing CAEFBD. He even takes the time to request an appointment with his supervisor—not necessarily because it's difficult to get in to see the supervisor, rather because Marvin wants to signal the importance of his proposal. The conversation during the meeting will probably go something like this.

"Well, Marvin, I've reviewed the proposal and I like what you say here about C. I also think this part at the end, these things you say about D are important. But I'm not sure what all this in the middle is."

Then Marvin responds, "I think you've hit the nail on the head, sir. C and D is where it's all at—they're really the key to the whole proposal. But you surely remember your boss talking about EF so I think we'd better give that some attention. And A and B are just some of the glue that hold it all together. All things considered, I think we should get moving on CAEFBD right away."

The supervisor then says, "I agree. But first we'll need final approval from my boss."

This is no problem because Marvin expected it from the beginning. The proposal then goes to the second level of management for review, and a meeting with Marvin and his supervisor's boss is scheduled. The conversation in this meeting will probably go something like this.

"Marvin, I'm pleased that somebody out there finally realized that EF is important to our organization, but why are you proposing all this other stuff?"

Then Marvin says, "JB, I think EF is the core of everything—one of the central priorities we're facing. It's the keystone to future success. In order to make it all happen though, we've got to dress it up a little. I think that CD is the cost effective way to do it at my supervisor's level and AB will help things a bit from my perspective. Accordingly, I think we should get moving on CAEFBD immediately."

"Do it!"

Now let's briefly analyze what Marvin has done. Has he compromised his own priorities or copped out? Is he guilty of apple polishing? Is this too sneaky or manipulative?

First off Marvin has *not* compromised his own priorities or copped out. His objectives (AB) will be achieved faster and with more support from upper management than if he had handled them any other way. Rather than get caught up in a win-lose competition with his two higher levels of management, he created a win-win (or "I win only if you win, we all win together) situation. Because they have more power Marvin is in much better shape with them both supporting CAEFBD than he would be in a three-horse race with AB, CD, and EF competing.

Secondly, Marvin is not guilty of apple polishing. Every member of the organization has a responsibility to support the rest of the organization in the achievement of their management objectives. There is an ever-stronger responsibility to support the higher levels of management. Making upper levels of management truly look good is not apple polishing—it's a fundamental responsibility of corporate employment.

And finally, were Marvin's actions too sneaky or manipulative? Hardly. Taking the time to do your homework, to find out what your boss and his boss want, then delivering it is far from being manipulative in any kind of negative sense. It's being responsible. And responsible employees and managers will always try to keep track of their own priorities and objectives and integrate them with organization priorities and objectives in such a way that neither suffers. In the final analysis, camels really are okay.

TIME FACTORS IN DECISION MAKING

There is a widespread belief in most U.S. organizations that everything should be done as quickly as possible. Frequently this emphasis on speed overshadows all other considerations, including quality.

A commonly heard expression among frustrated American workers and managers is, "That's typical of things around here . . . we never have time to do things right the first time, but always have time to do them over!" It's a trap we all fall into from time to time. For whatever reason, there is a common tendency among American managers to accept and attempt to implement half-baked solutions to problems and poorly staffed decisions rather than take the time in advance to develop higher quality courses of action at the outset. The norm is to take the shortcut that turns out to be the long cut in the long run.

Noted management theorist Peter F. Drucker, and Stanford University professor William G. Ouchi, have completed research identifying several distinct contrasts between the decision-making practices of U.S. and Japanese managers. The contrasts exist not only in differing approaches toward making decisions, but more importantly, in the consequences achieved. To best understand the differences between U.S. and Japanese decision-making practices, it is important to first understand the boundaries of decision-making activity. Decision-making activity, or the decision-making process, includes all activity which occurs from the time the need for a decision is identified until the chosen course of action is implemented.

Decision-making activity is divided into two categories of activity—the initial group of activities leading up to the actual election of a course of action (the decision phase), and the final group of activities associated with implementing the course of action (the action phase). The process can be shown as follows.

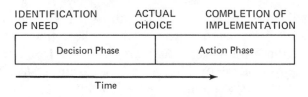

FIGURE 2-2. Phases of Decision-Making Activity.

The major differences between U.S. and Japanese managers is the point in the process at which the actual choice of alternatives takes place. U.S. decision makers push to decide sooner. This results in a shorter Decision Phase and a longer Action Phase for their decision-making processes. Japanese managers do the opposite. They make their choice much later in the process. This gives Japanese managers a much longer Decision Phase and a much shorter Action Phase in comparison. However, there is an additional important difference. By doing it their way, the Japanese complete the entire process in a shorter period of time. Although the typical U.S. manager may feel a greater sense of accomplishment sooner, this feeling generally turns out to be a deception. When viewed with objectivity, the typical Japanese decision will achieve implementation sooner, as shown below.

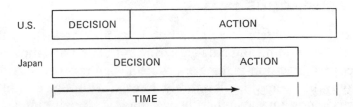

FIGURE 2-3. Comparison of U.S. and Japanese Decision Making.

The Japanese spend large amounts of time initially trying to understand the question—gaining insight into what will and what won't be affected by the decision. Everyone who will be affected by the decision is given the opportunity to make input. Data is gathered meticulously, analyzed, and evaluated. When a decision is finally made, however, it is implemented with startling speed and efficiency.

U.S. managers, on the other hand, press to make the decision as early as possible, usually demonstrating a very low tolerance for ambiguity. They tend to choose a course of action without thinking it through nearly as clearly or in as much detail as the Japanese. The result is confusion during implementation, constant shifting of direction and priorities, and frustration on the part of the people who are relied on to produce results. In short, the total process ends up taking longer and generally produces a lower quality result.

As the margin for error decreases, and the need in industry for efficient decision making increases, it is becoming more important for us to improve our performance. A comparison between U.S. and Japanese productivity since 1950 indicates our methods may be letting us down. In 1950, Japan required seven workers to achieve the same productivity as a single U.S. worker. By 1970 the ratio had diminished to 2 to 1. Since both countries have benefited comparably from technological improvements, most experts feel the reason we are losing ground is because of our less efficient management.

Managers must be decisive. They can't be afraid to take action when action is called for. However, acting too soon rarely saves time over the long run. Achieving the kind of timeliness in decision making and problem solving that results in optimum economy and efficiency is one of the key challenges confronting today's decision makers.

THE RELATIONSHIP BETWEEN FACTS AND ASSUMPTIONS

Most texts on problem solving and decision making identify the activities of fact finding and data gathering as the first and most important step in the decision-making or problem-solving process. Although this may at first seem valid, it is rarely the case. Although accurate fact finding is important, it can hardly overshadow effective implementation in degree of importance, and *rarely does a manager who makes sound, effective decisions start with the facts.* Invariably, top-notch decision-making and problem-solving processes begin with assumptions and opinions.

In spite of the old management adage that to assume is to incur unnecessary risk (ASSUME and it will make an "ASS of U & ME"), good managers understand there is a relationship between assumptions and reality that must be considered if they are going to come close to hitting the target of success with their decisions.

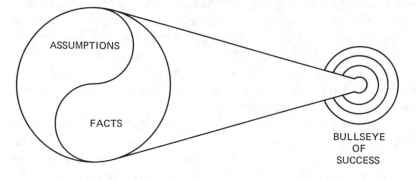

FIGURE 2–4. Relationship between Facts and Assumptions.

It is impossible to start with the facts without also starting out with some set of assumptions. To ask a person to do otherwise would be asking them to do the impossible. A person's assumptions establish the criteria in their own mind for what is relevant and what is not.

Managers who ignore their own personal opinions and assumptions invariably pay the price and achieve inferior results.

However, one must recognize that in order to avoid being tripped up by inappropriate assumptions, it is important to assume things consciously rather than unconsciously. This enables continuous testing and checking of the assumptions to be certain they remain valid. A manager who fails to do this is likely to experience a far higher level of frustration than one who doesn't. To illustrate the point, attempt the following exercise.

> Draw four connected lines, without retracing your path, that pass once through all the points below.

> •   •   •
>
> •   •   •
>
> •   •   •

If one of your assumptions was that the lines could not extend beyond the boundaries, this assumption prevented effective solution of the problem. Because the facts (dots) presented were tangible and visible, they caused you to lose sight of your assumptions and to fail.

Effectively solving the problem, as is the case with most management problems, relies upon being able to adjust the assumptions as the data dictates (within the parameters of accuracy). In reviewing the relationship between facts and opinions, renowned professor of management, Peter F. Drucker states the following:

> The effective decision-maker also knows that he starts out with opinions anyhow. The only choice he has is between using opinions as a productive factor in the decision-making process and deceiving himself into a false objectivity. People do not start out with the search for facts. They start out with an opinion. There is nothing wrong with this. People experienced in an area should be expected to

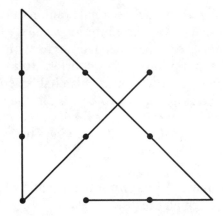

have an opinion. Not to have an opinion after having been exposed to an area for a good long time would argue an unobservant eye and a sluggish mind.

Management, 1973

However, it is also important to note the distinct difference between assumptions and expectations. Opinions and assumptions lend themselves to hypothetical testing. Expectations tend to cloud one's thinking by creating an anticipatory attitude that will tend to encourage one to look for the facts that support the expectation rather than the facts that will truly describe the reality of things. Further, it is important that after data are collected to find out what the facts are, the problem definition should be reevaluated and the objectives reviewed to ascertain current validity.

Both facts and assumptions should be translated into hypotheses which then are tested (not argued) to find the true reality of things as they relate to the decision or problem under scrutiny. The only expectation should be that our opinions and the things we know as facts will interact with each other and continue to change as we approach the Bullseye of Success.

Recent research is beginning to provide helpful insights about how this interaction between facts and assumptions affects judgments people make. The specific thought processes used in this area are called heuristic, which are simply methods for interpreting and reducing complex situations into simple frameworks so a judgment can be made. Most often people use these heuristic processes unconsciously.

In other words, they tend to build a framework for tackling a problem without being consciously aware of all the assumptions that are contributing to the structure.

It is this unconscious "simplification" of the task that causes most people to miss the solution to the nine dots and four lines problem on pages 31 and 32. The heuristic that gets most people into trouble there is the representative heuristic. The representative heuristic operates in a way that causes people to assign an idea, task, problem, event, or object to one category rather than another because its features resemble something familiar in that category. In this case, the dots resembled a box. Because of this many people unfortunately reduce the problem to the apparently more simple task of making the lines fit the box rather than the more complex task of comparing the lines to nine dots. Matching four to one seems easier than matching four to nine.

Although reducing thought processes to simpler form is absolutely essential in almost all our activities, when done wrong it gets us in deep trouble. Applying heuristics improperly, as is frequently done when done unconsciously, can lead us astray, substantially limiting effectiveness in problem solving and decision making.

There are a number of other heuristics that frequently cause managers to err. For example, the availability heuristic causes objects or events to be judged as frequent or probable or infrequent or improbable on the basis of how readily pertinent examples enter the mind of the person who is making the judgment. For example, assume you were to ask two managers to state their views regarding the overall threat of unionism to management's ability to successfully manage the country's major corporations. Assume one manager worked in a company with no unions and the other worked in a company with aggressive union representation. Most likely you'd hear two very different evaluations of the situation. Their assessment of the broader problem would be dramatically affected as they reduced this complex issue to terms they could relate to, which in this case would be their personal experience. This is the most readily available data they have to draw on, thus their judgment will be directly affected. Without taking time to look at the facts, the answers of both may be irrelevant to the real question.

Another nemesis to managers is the covariation heuristic. Typically it causes problems when managers fail to appreciate the relationships between cause and effect, between strategies and results, or between early-warning indicators and later developing crises. For cause and effect situations which occur on an incident-by-incident basis the heuristic is usually more helpful than hindering. Over time, in related kinds of situations we learn that certain things relate to different things in special ways and we take this into account in our actions. An example of this is the relationship that a reasonable pay raise has with a worker's satisfaction. Give a worker a pay raise and it will almost always bring happiness and satisfaction (at least temporarily).

But the covariation heuristic can also cause problems, both by implying relationships where they don't exist or in failing to recognize relationships when they do exsit. When these misinterpretations affect a manager's understanding of the relationship between strategies and results they can be devastating. A frequent example of this occurs when a manager takes over a new position. New faces, new responsibilities, new challenges, and setting all create energy, enthusiasm, and success for the first few months. Exciting results ensue, validating in the manager's own mind that he or she is the right person for the job and is doing all the right things. But then something starts to happen. After several months things start to get harder. Results don't come as easily, problems arise, and schedules start slipping. The manager starts worrying and begins looking for the problem. Someone suggests using more formal and deliberate management techniques, which the manager considers. But the idea gets rejected or benefits from only a half-hearted attempt to use them. Fairly often this is the answer—the only viable strategy to get things back in shape and produce the desired result. But it is rejected because the manager reflects back to the time when results were good and concludes that the application of all these techniques was not a factor, as they would not be helpful here. The manager recalls the good times when results were good and concludes that the management techniques in use at the time were what caused those results, ignoring the effect that the newness, excitement, and enthusiasm had in causing those results. Accordingly, the manager chooses a strategy that only compounds the problem, and grows increasingly more confused and frustrated.

It is important that informant, events, and circumstances be viewed and analyzed as accurately as possible if good management results are to be produced. Heuristics focus on how information is processed since it is acquired, but the actual acquisition of information is equally important. Proper data-gathering techniques are essential for successful decision making and problem solving.

DATA GATHERING: ASKING THE RIGHT QUESTIONS

Contrary to some decision-making and problem-solving techniques, the Lyles Method does not treat data gathering as a separate and independent activity. Rather, data gathering is considered to be an ongoing and continuous task that supports each and every management action—it is essential to every step of decision making and problem solving.

The safest way to ensure reliable data is to develop reliable data-gathering techniques. Frequently when managers find they have acted on faulty data, they blame the source. Although this is sometimes appropriate, more often than not the true blame rests with the information seeker who simply asked the wrong questions in the first place.

Trained investigators learn early on how important it is to ask the right questions. What is asked and how they ask it can make a substantial difference in the type and quality of data they eventually accumulate. Accordingly, they spend a great deal of time learning how to ask relevant and effective questions. They also spend time reviewing their practices and testing new approaches. Managers would do well to take heed from their example. A manager's long-term success could very well hinge upon the ability to gather relevant information in a timely fashion and in a format which lends itself to appropriate action.

Before looking at the questions themselves, however, it is important to decide upon the basic orientation to choose for data-gathering activities. There are two general approaches to choose from. The first involves setting aside all preliminary notions or preconceived ideas regarding the facts and conducting a very wide open investigation. In this approach everything is considered to be relevant until it is proven to be irrelevant. The second approach involves making explicit assumptions about what the data might look like, and then forming a series of hypotheses to be tested during the investigation, comparing assumptions against reality as new facts are uncovered. Both approaches are valid, depending upon the specific circumstances at hand. The type of questions asked, however, will be significantly different for each.

A common belief among managers used to be that a key factor in determining success of decision-making or problem-solving efforts was the intuitive abilities of the individual manager. It was thought that those capable of greater intuitive insights would naturally outperform those with lesser intuitive ability. It was further believed that intuitive traits were inherited rather than developed. Thus, some people had the natural gifts necessary for good management and others didn't, and those who didn't were out of luck because there was no way to develop these genetically derived traits.

More recently, however, much of this has been proven false. Most of the intellectual traits previously believed to be genetically derived have now been proven to be attainable through the accepted processes of learning. A profound example is in the area of intuition. Formerly thought to occur through the mysterious and incomprehensible processes of the occult, at least one aspect of this ability has been defined as having the ability to reconstruct remote events.

Most events (including problems) for which the manager is held accountable take place at a location removed from that of the manager. Success then depends upon the manager being able to reconstruct that event (whether past, present, or future) to be able to respond to the demands of the situation with accuracy. Data gathering, or more specifically the ability to ask the right questions, is the tool used to carry out this process efficiently. Being able to reconstruct remote events can alleviate the need for a manager to rely solely upon intuition as the basis for decision making and problem solving.

THE ABILITY TO RECONSTRUCT REMOTE EVENTS

Assume for a moment that a problem arose during the time you were away from the office attending a course. Upon completion of the course you return to your place of work and become aware of the fact that a problem arose and of the need to take corrective action. The first thing you must do, of course, is define the problem—to find out what happened. This means you must implement some type of data-gathering strategy that will lead to one outcome—a picture in your mind of the event that occurred away from you. It is now remote in both space and time, but the need for you to take action (which could include doing nothing) confronts you now. You must reconstruct that remote event to a sufficient degree of detail that will allow you to act in the appropriate manner. An important distinction here is that you don't need all the data, simply enough data to allow you to take the appropriate action.

It would be nice if you could have had a videotape machine to record visually and in full sound everything that happened. All you would then have to do is to press the replay button and everything would be presented to you, perhaps even in living color. Or almost everything would be presented. You would still miss the tone and climate the events took place in, and of course you wouldn't be able to record what everyone was thinking. Nor would you be able to witness every possible event that occurred previously that could have led up to this problem or event. Play this game for awhile and it's easy to see that it would be almost impossible to devise any kind of tracking system that would provide for total instant replay. Accordingly, managers must rely on their individual wisdom, experience, and knowledge to sort out what is important and collect data that is relevant to the situation.

Reconstructing remote events is a little like playing the old television game of Concentration. In that game, a contestant would use memory, knowledge, and a bit of luck to match two squares which would then be turned to reveal two parts of a puzzle that was hidden behind the board. This process of revealing parts of the puzzle or jingle continued until enough of it was exposed to allow the contestant to guess what it was.

For a manager, the process is similar. First is the assumption that there is a picture (or puzzle). The questioning or data-gathering process is the means used to add meaning to the puzzle or to give insight into the event that occurred. Experience and technical or content knowledge enable the manager to know which questions to ask, or what data might be relevant in a particular situation. The probe continues until enough of the critical elements of the problem are revealed so the manager can act on the problem with a reasonable level of confidence. It works like this.

First the manager finds out something happened.

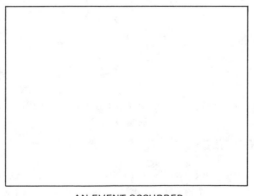

AN EVENT OCCURRED

Although data is scarce, the manager begins to fill in the blanks and learns more about the situation. Each bit of data becomes an additional piece of the puzzle.

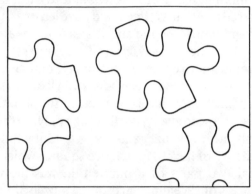

FACTS SURROUNDING THE EVENT ARE UNCOVERED

It is important to note here that the more the manager learns the more the manager knows about the unknown. If the knowledge gathered through data collection is represented by the area contained within each piece of the puzzle, then the perimeter of each piece represents the manager's interface with the unknown. The more the manager knows, the more the manager will know about the unknown.

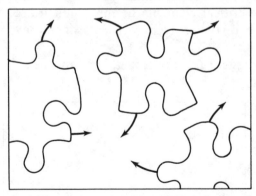

PERIMETERS GIVE INSIGHTS INTO THE UNKNOWN

GATHERING RELEVANT DATA

In order to reconstruct events or create a picture in your mind descriptive of the situation, it is necessary to ask questions likely to produce a meaningful representation. There are four categories of questions to be used in this process. Each category is presented below with samples of the types of questions that would be most productive in defining the problem or situation.

WHAT IS THE *NATURE* OF THE PROBLEM OR DECISION?

1. Is it people, operational, or technical?
2. Does it pertain to a particular functional specialty such as marketing, engineering, distribution, or finance?
3. Are the variables tangible and specific or intangible?

HOW *VISIBLE* OR INTENSELY FELT IS THE PROBLEM?

1. Does *everyone* who should, realize that a problem exists?
2. Are they ready to confront the problem, decide on a course of action, and then act?
3. Do they understand the significance of the problem? (And does their understanding match yours?)
4. Can tangible problem indicators be identified?
5. Is the problem clear to all?
6. Is the problem significant, or minor?
7. Is the problem routine, or unusual?
8. Is the problem urgent, or not urgent?
9. What other problems or decisions are competing for attention?
10. Should priorities be adjusted to address this problem or decision?

WHAT IS THE *SCOPE* OF THIS PROBLEM OR DECISION IN RELATION TO TIME, CONDITIONS, AND ORGANIZATION?

1. Is this an old problem?
2. What actions have been taken previously?
3. What has been learned from past experiences?
4. What have other organizations done in similar situations?
5. What formal knowledge (from books, journals, expert opinions) can be applied in this situation?
6. Are there still unexplained factors from the past?
7. What operations are affected?
8. What operations are *not* affected?
9. What different conditions exist now compared to the past?

10. What people are primarily involved or affected?
11. What sections of the organization are affected?
12. What is the effect on outsiders, such as customers, clients, or vendors?
13. What effect will there be in the future?
14. What other decisions or problems are related to this situation?

HOW *IMPORTANT* IS THE ISSUE AT HAND?

1. How is this affecting the achievement of organizational goals and objectives?
2. What are the long- and short-range consequences?
3. How did the problem initially gain recognition?
4. Did the issue arise naturally as a consequence of regular organizational activity?
5. If introduced by one person, what was that person's motivation for introducing it?
6. Is the problem clearly related to operating needs?
7. What is at stake organizationally?
8. Who has an interest in the problem?
9. What is at stake for each person who has an interest? (Consider both gains and losses.)
10. Who are the controlling personalities?
11. What are the political implications of the issue?
12. Are people likely to react in predictable ways no matter what course of action is adopted?
13. Is the situation competitive? In other words can you expect someone to try to counter your moves or to act independently of anything you might do?
14. Does the situation point to some weakness someone else may at this time be trying to exploit?
15. What do you, personally, stand to gain or lose from this situation?

RESULTS: THE MOST IMPORTANT FACTOR

Stories abound of managers who failed because they were more loyal to their method than to the bottom line. A fail-safe system for any area of management activity has yet to have been devised. Accordingly, the

Lyles Method is presented in this context. The overall approach is characterized to the maximum extent possible to contain both structure and flexibility.

Structure is provided in the form of a seven-step procedure to be used when attacking problems of all sorts. The phases of activity comprising those seven steps are universally applied to all problems.

Flexibility is provided in the form of strategy options—different ways to carry out problem-solving and decision-making activities depending on the situation. The strategies are diverse enough to provide an almost limitless variety of approaches.

This is important because no two problems of management are ever the same. The only constant that remains the same from problem to problem, decision to decision, is the need to produce the right result for that particular situation. After all, that is the basis upon which each manager's performance is evaluated. If there was "one best way" to achieve optimum results in every situation it would have been discovered long ago and everyone would be using it today. But there isn't. There is no one best way.

However, by understanding a number of different ways to approach different problems it is possible to increase the likelihood that better results will be produced over the long run. It is the intent here to present viable alternatives and justification for choosing them, remembering that in the final analysis the results are what count most.

3
Overall Strategy

Just as an army would not proceed into battle without a battle plan, or an athletic team would not enter the competition without a game plan, a manager should not accept the challenge of a serious problem or decision without a planned method of approach. And like the field commander or coach, the more options the manager carries into the fray, the more likely success will be achieved. An army commander who has air forces, artillary, tanks, and diverse weaponry to use during battle is much more likely to succeed than the commander with only infantry. The same is true of the football team capable of passing, kicking, and taking advantage of special team opportunities as well as running. And so it can be said of the manager who has the skill and capability to show flexibility in approach and method when attacking different kinds of problems and decisions in the struggle to achieve meaningful organization results. Because the problems of modern-day management are so diverse, the issues surrounding them complex, it is invaluable for a manager to have just as diverse a range of options with which to respond.

Strategies, when considered and applied on two levels, will provide this diversity. The first level is *overall strategies,* which is the focus of this chapter. The second level is *process strategies.* These are different strategies to be used in each of the seven phases of the Lyles Method for decision making and problem solving. Detailed presentations of all the process strategies are presented in Chapters 4 through 10 along with the step in the Method in which they are applied. The guidelines for using the process strategies are fairly specific and detailed.

The overall strategies, however, are clearly more general and much broader in scope. The major concern related to overall strategies (which is also a concern related to the use of process strategies) is the concern of use. The strategies, like any other tool or aid, only work when they are used. Just like any competency or capability, the easiest and surest way to true proficiency is practice combined with critique. It is best to start practicing and experimenting with the routine problems and the relatively insignificant decisions. Address them formally, and develop the habit of making strategy decisions consciously. Then go back and critique. Try several different approaches and see where they lead. Determine which worked best and what kind of approaches produce the highest quality results for you with different kinds of problems. Everyone is different, so what works best for one person may not be the most desirable method for another. Take the time to develop reasonably good abilities and good habits when handling small problems and decisions. Then when the less frequent but more important ones come along you'll be better prepared and much more comfortable. You'll have greater confidence, and it will be easier to make the right choices and pursue effective strategies than it will be to choose the wrong ones or be forced to "muddle through."

CONSIDERATIONS FOR SELECTING STRATEGIES

The most important principle of strategy selection is that the strategy should fit the circumstances. To best choose such a strategy, a manager first must have some sense of what things are important to consider when assessing different circumstances. A number of important parameters accompany each situation that provide the basis for judgment to determine which strategies are most likely to produce the best results for the moment. These include such things as time constraints, urgency, risk, cost, cost effectiveness, importance to those affected, the need for quality, and importance to the organization. Before acting on any but the most obvious and routine problems and decisions, the manager should make an assessment of these fundamental considerations in order to use them as a basis on which all other management action is taken.

In order to develop the habit of taking these factors into consideration, it is helpful to use a formal method or approach initially. It would
be naive at best to assume all managers would use a formal checklist
each time they were confronted with a new problem. However, it is
very helpful to use such a checklist for at least a few weeks, then
periodically thereafter, to first instill these factors in the problem-
solving and decision-making processes and then to refresh the memory, providing reinforcement at later times. To this end, the following
checklist of strategy considerations should be helpful.

STRATEGY CONSIDERATIONS CHECKLIST		
TIME CONSTRAINTS	NONE ———————	URGENT
POTENTIAL COSTS	LOW ———————	HIGH
POTENTIAL PAYOFF	LOW ———————	HIGH
VISIBILITY	LOW ———————	HIGH
RISK TO COMPANY	LOW ———————	HIGH
RISK TO MANAGER (ME)	LOW ———————	HIGH
IMPORTANCE TO COMPANY	LOW ———————	HIGH
IMPORTANCE TO MANAGER	LOW ———————	HIGH
IMPORTANCE TO OTHERS	LOW ———————	HIGH
NEED FOR QUALITY	LOW ———————	HIGH
NEED FOR ACCEPTANCE	LOW ———————	HIGH

It is easy to get caught up in the dilemma of assuming or deliberately
determining that for the decision or problem of the moment every item
on the checklist is critically important. In other words, to exaggerate
just a little, there is a temptation to assume that each problem, when it
is being considered, must be resolved today; has overwhelming cost implications for the operation or organization; is the most important
issue of the day to the work force and to top management; and has absolutely no margin for error. Let's briefly examine some of the realities
surrounding actual problems managers encounter.

First is the consideration of time and urgency. Urgency has nothing
to do with overall importance. The reverse is also true. Many important problems benefit substantially from a realistic and reasonable
amount of waiting time. Not all problems can afford to be put off, but
most can. And when they are put off a number of things are likely to

occur. Quite frequently they go away—they either resolve themselves, or someone else resolves them, or the circumstances change so they are no longer important. The next most likely occurrence is that those responsible will have the opportunity for exposure to more data and deeper thinking that will inevitably lead to better and more productive results. Sometimes the problem will escalate creating more concern on the part of more people, thus helping to establish a climate more supportive of the manager's problem-solving and decision-making efforts. Occasionally, (more often with technical problems than with operational or people problems) the problem will reach true crisis proportions and go out of control. This is the only danger inherent in waiting rather than rushing into problems, and should be carefully guarded against. But all in all, it is far better to move deliberately with well-planned efforts than to rush in because of a perceived sense of urgency.

When considering cost factors, the most important thing to do is to be specific. If there is one area of management responsibilities in which managers tend to get vague and ambiguous, it's the area of cost. This is probably because the more specific one gets when discussing costs, the more specific one can also get regarding individual accountability. Eventually someone has to pay for it from their own budget. Things to avoid when considering cost are cop-outs such as, "Well, cost isn't really an issue here because we've got to do it anyway," or, "We can't really estimate the costs involved here until we get into it." It is easy to get caught up in the "if it's a good idea it's worth doing" syndrome. It is only worth doing if the benefit outweighs the cost. A problem is only worth solving if the benefit to solving it outweighs the cost of not solving it. A decision is only worth making if the resulting benefit from the decision outweighs the cost. However, how much gets spent in solving a problem or making a decision can be changed—as can the quality of outcome. Sometimes better decisions are arrived at through greater expenditures of effort and funds. So before doing anything the manager should ascertain what the stakes are for the current situation being considered. Obviously, for a decision that could affect millions of dollars of profits, the manager would not select a haphazard strategy. Nor does it make sense to spend thousands of dollars deciding an issue whose only consequence is in the neighborhood of ten or twenty dollars. These examples are obvious. But the difficult determinations are the ones that lie in between these extremes. It is an unfortunate fact of management that it is in this middle hazy area that most management problems and decisions exist. It is essential then, that as a preliminary step, these factors are assessed and the highest level of specificity be aspired to.

Quality is another dimension frequently misunderstood, misinterpreted, and misrepresented. It is not essential that every decision of management, and every solution to every problem be of the highest possible quality. It is only necessary that they be of acceptable quality—of high enough quality to get the desired result. If you are talking about quality relative to a specific quality or service, that is one thing. Quality in that sense has a completely different meaning and can usually be measured in an absolute sense. For example, if you compare two pairs of shoes that are different, one will most definitely have a better quality than the other, and these differences could be very important to a potential buyer. For a manager, however, few decisions require the very best quality. At least 75% require only a minimum level of so-called "quality" to produce the desired results. To expend energy and resources beyond this level is wasteful and unnecessary, even though people do it all the time. Take the case of the manager attending a recent seminar who was given an hour to solve a particularly challenging marketing problem. He tackled it enthusiastically and, at the end of the exercise (in the time allowed) he told what his answers were and how he arrived at them. He was told he was correct. However, in the discussion that followed he observed that he "really needed two days to solve the problem right" rather than the one hour he was given. Even though he had exactly the right answer after spending an hour on the problem, he was firmly convinced he could still develop a much higher quality answer by expending sixteen times the effort. Quality in decision making and problem solving means developing the most cost-effective method to produce the desired short- and long-range results.

Impact is another important consideration. Having the right answer is not enough if it adversely affects either operations or the people in the organization. N.R.F. Meier was first to point out the need for both quality and acceptability in decisions. In other words, the best solution obtainable is worth nothing if the people who will be depended on to produce the final result don't accept it. Recently a West Coast manufacturer of industrial equipment provided an interesting example of how good decisions can break down when impact is not adequately assessed prior to implementation. The company sold one of its major

OVERALL STRATEGY   47

product lines to an industrial equipment manufacturer on the East Coast. On the surface the deal looked like a transaction sent from heaven. The product line was top quality, state-of-the-art equipment. However, the West Coast company was running into difficulty because the market for the equipment was just outside their well-established market where they had a good reputation and a lot of experience. Although the East Coast company lacked the depth of technical expertise in this particular area, the product was perfect for their market. By buying the product line they would not only get a good product they could exploit, they would also get along with it, the technical staff, and therefore the depth of expertise, they needed to be able to represent the product. All factors considered, a good deal for both companies. However, no one considered the internal impact of the decision. None of the critically needed software specialists or technicians were at all excited about moving from the West Coast to the East Coast. When the purchasing company came to the selling company to interview the employees, they handled it poorly. They projected an attitude that indicated they thought everyone should jump at the chance to come work for them without showing much concern at all for the employees. The result fell just short of disaster. All the software specialists and technicians joined together and announced they would not go along with the deal. Panic set in, and the deal was almost completely botched. Had it been, everyone would have ended up on the losing end. Finally, however, after a great amount of negotiating, arguing, and discussing, emotions were brought back under control and the deal was completed. There can be no doubt, however, that the results were far less positive than they would have been had the decision makers taken into account the impact of their decision on the people prior to taking action.

As Meier has said in many of his works, overall effectiveness is a function of both quality and acceptance. The best quality is worth absolutely nothing if not accepted by those who will be affected. The following equation shows the relationship.

$$EFFECTIVENESS = f(QUALITY \times ACCEPTANCE)$$

It is possible to have a decision rated 100% on the quality scale, as the decision of the industrial manufacturers was, and if the acceptance of those who must do it is 0, have the decision be totally ineffective. One hundred times zero is zero. And the same is true of the reverse. It is possible, although less likely, that everyone could have complete acceptance times zero (for the wrong answer) is still zero.

Accordingly, one of the challenges of problem solving and decision making is to achieve the highest possible values for both sides of the equation. This is where strategies can be of tremendous value.

THE FIRST DECISION OF STRATEGY

The first and foremost question a decision maker should ask when confronted with a problem is, should I or should I not take on the responsibilty of responding to this issue. "To Act, or Not To Act," that is the primary question when new problems and questions arise. Consider the shipping company that for twenty years was plagued with the staffing problem of filling a certain high-level staff position that became vacant quite frequently. During the twenty-first year a new president was hired from outside the company. The problem position again became vacant and the president was asked how he would like to go about filling the position. He responded by asking what would happen if the position were not filled. After investigation, his staff said the answer was nothing. They discovered the position was created to carry out duties that had been obsolete for over a dozen years.

Doing nothing is more than merely one alternative. It is the first alternative to be considered, and should always be considered before all others. It should be considered before any serious expenditure of time and energy devoted to any other aspects of a problem. The decision to act should be the conscious and deliberate one. If there is an underlying assumption regarding a manager's intentions, that assumption should be that no action will be taken unless the need for action has been clearly and forcefully established.

Confusion exists in the minds of many managers regarding what it means to be decisive and to act quickly. There is a big difference between rushing into problems and decisions where no need exists and moving quickly to implement a plan of action in an area of critical need. The big difference is between managing toward some set of goals, objectives, or long-range organizational purpose, and managing by crisis and reaction to every "urgent" perturbation of the day. Decisiveness only counts when it results in a measurable and meaningful contribution to the achievement of a manager's objectives.

Without this, no matter how ego-gratifying or self-satisfying the activity may be, it is meaningless. The strong manager will not be afraid to ignore the "urgent" problems of little consequence, saving energy and time to devote to the implementation of truly meaningful plans that will naturally absorb a tremendous amount of effort anyway.

The most practical way to develop this habit of consciously deciding whether or not to act is to remember to ask three questions when new decisions and problems arise.

1. What would happen if I ignored it?
2. Is action warranted?
3. Is now the best time to confront this issue?

The first question is valuable because it focuses on results. When asking this question, it is important to look at both the positive and negative outcomes that are possible and likely. Consider the warehouse manager who observed a dispute between two relatively mature shipping supervisors who worked for him. The problem was serious enough to temporarily disrupt work. Most managers would respond to their immediate impulse and rush over, intervene, and attempt to solve the problem. In this case, however, the warehouse manager stopped himself, and reflected on possible outcomes if he ignored the problem and took no immediate action himself. He returned to work he could best accomplish by himself and left the supervisors alone. After a short time they worked out the difference of opinion themselves. The result was increased productivity on the part of the warehouse manager, and the two supervisors having learned something about solving problems among themselves. All of them and the organization will be better off in the future.

The second question, "Is action warranted?" is important because it brings into focus such factors as justification and cost. Another variation of this question is, "Is it worth it?" Whether or not the stereotype is justified, government agencies have a reputation for being penny-wise and pound-foolish in this regard, forever solving problems that simply are not worth solving. An example is the state regulatory board that was told at one of its bimonthly meetings that a private organization had failed to submit an administrative report that was required by regulation some nine months previous. Members of the remiss organization told the board that in the midst of starting a new program they had simply forgotten to submit the report. This was also verified by board staff. Other than the fact that the report was required by regulations, there was no observable purpose that anyone on the board or the board staff could describe for the report. The head of the board, however, directed that two state employees on the board staff travel four hundred miles to the remiss organization to determine if they could find out more about why the report was not submitted and to determine what could be done in the future to ensure the same thing didn't happen again! They were further directed to make a full report at the next board meeting so the board could determine whether new policy might be needed to prevent similar occurrences in the future. All this for a report that had not been used, that no one had missed for nine months, and no one could define a use for. The board members' most common complaint was that they simply did not have enough time to do everything required of them. It is obvious their problem, like most governmental entities, was not insufficient time. They were simply spending their time addressing problems and issues that were irrelevant.

The solution the state board in the previous paragraph was aiming toward is called the Bureaucratic Solution, and will be referred to later in the book. The Bureaucratic Solution is any solution that consists of writing a new policy, regulation, or law to solve a problem that has occurred once, and will almost certainly not recur. It is the lazy way to save face in management. The manager, or someone in the manager's area of responsibility makes a mistake that should have been avoided or would have been avoided had the person or people involved been using common sense at the time. The mistake gets made, and because it was, simply stated, a mistake, the potential for embarrassment is present. To avoid this the manager reports the problem as a weakness or shortcoming in existing policy. Rather than say, "I made a mistake," or, "One of my people made a mistake," the manager says, "We've got a problem here that was caused because we don't have a policy that tells people what to do in situations like this. We'd better get something out in writing in a hurry so we can avoid similar problems in the future." Of course, the underlying assumption is that people aren't supposed to be able to think and apply common sense, so every possible situation has to be covered by some kind of policy document or regulation. And the end result is that people don't think for themselves, efficiency becomes much harder to maintain, and productivity becomes an irrelevant term. Stay away from the Bureaucratic Solution. Make people or circumstances convince you in every instance that action is warranted and justified. And don't take action unless it is imperative that you do so.

The third question, "Is now the best time to confront this issue?" brings to light another dimension to problem solving that can inadvertently have a profound effect on the final results. Frequently the very best solutions to problems fail because they were put forth at the wrong time. Jennifer D. learned this the hard way. As a production supervisor at a medium-sized manufacturing company, she was constantly under the gun to meet production schedules. To do her job better, she finally managed to get her boss to sit down with her and establish specific performance standards and goals on a daily, weekly, and monthly basis. This was difficult at first, because she manufactured several products on her line and production loads were hard to predict. After a few false starts, things finally started to fall into place. Both felt they had forecasts and schedules that were realistic and manageable. The month started well, and by the end of the first week, things were going according to plan. Then on Monday afternoon of the second week, Jennifer's boss came to her with an urgent request for her people to do some modifications on previously manufactured products. Although relatively small, they were enough to cause her tight schedule to slip. She was irritated, but didn't say anything. Just before lunch on Tuesday her boss brought in some more special projects that needed to be completed on an urgent basis. This caused more of a disruption in her work flow and upset her considerably, but she still avoided saying anything to her boss, trying to do her best. Then in midafternoon on Wednesday it all broke loose. Her boss brought in still another special project. There was no way she could possibly complete all three "specials" and still maintain the previously agreed upon production schedule. She lost her temper, telling her boss how wrong it was for him to bring these specials to her, knowing that with the agreed upon schedule it would be impossible to do both. This angered her boss, who responded by telling her that she should be able to do the work, and if she couldn't do it, maybe he would find someone who could. Each stormed off in a different direction, angered at what the other had said.

Although it is easy in this type of problem to take sides and say who should have done what, the bottom line is one of timing. Jennifer had a right to be upset. Her irritation was natural and could have been predicted. On the other hand, her boss almost certainly had legitimate reason to make the requests he made. And although he could have been more effective had he handled it differently, his reaction was understandable. After all, he was most likely responding to demands from higher level management and all the pressures he was experiencing to perform. The key is timing. Had Jennifer simply chosen a different time to confront the problem, the results would probably have been quite different. At the time he brought the third special request she should have simply said, "O.K., I'll do my best." This would have conveyed to him she was being supportive and that she cared about doing a good job. Then she should have taken some time to organize her thoughts, and sometime later, maybe near the end of the shift or at the beginning of the next work day, asked him if they could meet to talk about some concerns she had regarding her job. His interpretation of her motives at this time would likely be much different. He would be much more likely to think she was genuinely concerned about doing a good job under these circumstances than the other. In the other circumstances it was easy for him to interpret her statements as a reaction to being asked to do work—and he therefore felt able to disregard her statements, taking them as a sign she was just being emotional over work she didn't want to do.

When they sat down to talk, she should then have said something like, "Last week we laid out the monthly production schedules. For the first week everything went perfect. On Monday, however, you brought me specials that began to disrupt our plan. On Tuesday you brought me even more. And on Wednesday you brought still more. The result is my schedule is completely shot, and there is no way I can do everything we've agreed on. I'd like us to figure out some way we can organize the work so it will flow smoothly, in accordance with our plans." This would have set a completely different tone for the conversation. Jennifer's concerns would have a much better chance of being interpreted in a more favorable light for her. The message she wanted to get across would probably be conveyed. Tempers would be under control, so constructive communication would be more likely. This won't guarantee success, but the odds would surely be more in Jennifer's favor if she chose a time to confront the problem when her boss would probably listen to her seriously rather than considering her to be part of the problem.

In deciding whether or not to act on a problem or decision, there is one more major issue to be considered. All of a manager's actions should be congruent with existing policy and objectives. Extraordinary amounts of time are wasted in organizations by managers who, when confronted with problems and decisions, automatically assume they are the first to confront a situation of this type and charge ahead without looking around to see what guidance already exists in policy and operating manuals to cover the particular situation. Not only is this time consuming and slovenly managerial behavior, it is dangerous in many ways.

Policies and standard operation procedures bring benefit. There are distinct advantages to having uniformity in organizational functioning and in the behavior of its members. Consistency is hard enough to achieve when everyone in the organization knows and understands the policies and desired operating procedures and practices. It is almost an impossibility when guidelines are ignored. However, the consequences of ignoring them are of sufficient gravity that each and every manager should always first look to existing policy and regulations for guidance when confronted with problems and decisions of any great magnitude. The field of employee relations is one area where a multitude of problems exist because so many supervisors and managers take personnel actions, especially when disciplining subordinates, without regard to company policies and guidelines. The result is that arbitration boards interpret the actions taken to be the established practice rather than what is written in the company's policy manual. This causes disciplinary actions to be overturned, salary dollars to be spent undeservedly, and morale to be adversely affected.

Although serious, the personnel problems are minor compared to the problem encountered by the marketing-oriented company whose product line manager made a decision that was in the best interest of his own particular product line without considering the other product lines or the company as a whole. He nearly bankrupted another product line before top management realized what was happening. Had he consulted the company policy manual first, he would have discovered an already laid out and completely detailed plan for dealing with his problem. By following this plan he would have not only produced very lucrative results for his product line, but he would have also avoided the adverse effects on the rest of the company. And he would probably also still have his job.

Before acting on any problem or decision, a manager should first ask the following questions regarding policy.

1. Is this situation covered by existing policy?
2. How is policy affected?
3. How does the situation relate to current goals, objectives, and plans?

In asking these questions an important consideration should be kept in mind. If the policies conflict with the desired course of action, or if they stand in the way of being able to accomplish those things that are in the best interests of the organization, *the manager who first discovers this has the responsibility to confront the policy and initiate action to change it.* Policies should never be circumvented for the sake of expediency. If they are current and in force, they should be followed. If they are obsolete they should be dropped or eliminated. And, once again, the first person to determine the existence of obsolescence has the responsibility to see that changes are made.

THE SECOND STRATEGY DECISION: WHO SHOULD ACT?

Results quite frequently depend just as much upon who does the work as on any other factor. Yet quite often, managers select those to be involved in different decision-making and problem-solving activities rather arbitrarily. In most cases, this is the result of habit. For example, some managers prefer to keep things fairly close to their chest, so to speak. Accordingly, they do a lot of this kind of work themselves without soliciting much input or participation from others. On the other hand, some managers prefer to get as many people as possible involved in as many different activities as possible. In each case the manager is probably following the most comfortable course of action; one that has evolved over a number of years and is now followed out of habit. The only drawback is that although the manager will be most comfortable always doing things basically the same, the results must be inferior. The same approach simply cannot be the best strategy for every circumstance. Comfort does not equate to best.

Good managers avoid becoming a slave to their habits. If they foster habits, they are usually habits of flexibility and adaptability. Good managers are quick of mind and nimble when taking management action. They know that each situation they encounter is different in some way from the last. They will search to find that difference in order to develop first a strategy, and finally a solution that will be the best possible under the circumstances. When presented with a problem and asked what should be done, the good manager will most likely respond by saying, "It all depends," and proceed to ask more questions which will lead to a better understanding of the dilemma. Most important, the good manager won't be found locked in a rut, either in method or by using the same people over and over again while others remain in the background. To the contrary, over the long run an observer would note the good manager's use of multiple strategies and, equally as important, the use of every person available, drawing on their strengths as needed to solve the problems of the day. The following options exist for involving different people in decision-making and problem-solving activities.

Assign to the Most Qualified Person

When the need for high-quality results is crucial, and the expertise of the problem solver is likely to make a difference on the final outcome, this may be the wisest course of action. An advantage of this strategy, as with all strategies of delegation, is that someone else can do the work, then when it is completed, the manager is in a position to critique the result without getting bogged down in the problem itself. The major determination here is whether or not it is essential to assign the problem to the most qualified person. A rut many managers get stuck in is in always first looking to the better people when making assignments. A disadvantage of doing this is that the best people get better and the average or below average people tend to stagnate because they are denied the same opportunities for challenge and growth. Only make the assignment to the most qualified person when quality is the first and foremost criteria and cannot be compromised.

Assign to any Qualified Person

This means to establish a minimum level of expertise or ability required to adequately attack the problem or decision and then choose from the group of people who meet the minimum level of qualifications to take on the assignment. Although you might end up choosing the most qualified, chances are you would not. The advantage of this strategy over the previous one is that more people have an opportunity to take on a broader and more diverse scope of assignments, and the manager has a great deal more flexibility in supervising the work load to keep things flowing more smoothly. Although the results may not be the best in each individual case, they will get the job done and the total output of the work group will most probably be better than average. To use this strategy, however, one must first overcome the false belief that every problem and every decision requires a "best" solution. This is simply not so. What is required in each case is a solution that will get the job done and adequately meet the needs of the situation.

Do it Yourself

This strategy offers the advantage of complete control over the process and assures complete certainty of the nature of the outcome. It is used far too much by managers who don't trust their subordinates or are afraid of losing control. A distinct disadvantage of doing it yourself too often is that it takes time. It is usually best to delegate to someone else, then check their results, than to always rely on yourself, using your own time, and foregoing the possibility of a back-up person to check or critique the results. The best time to use this strategy is when a relatively simple problem or decision arises and is likely to have little noticeable consequence, and there are no major gains to be made through delegation or assignment. In these cases, the best thing to do is to act immediately, get it done and out of the way, and move on to more important things.

Assign Simultaneously to Two or More People
Who Will Act Independently

Although a slightly more costly strategy than some others, this approach may be appropriate under a number of different circumstances. Assume for a moment you were confronted with an operational problem that could conceivably be approached from either a production or a marketing perspective. A viable strategy might be to assign the problem simultaneously to a marketing expert and a production person to develop their solutions independent of each other. The result could be that you would benefit from the very best of each specialist's thinking without having them contaminate each other's thought processes. Another case might be the kind of technical problem that could conceivably be solved with two different types of technical expertise. In today's world of complicated technology this is becoming more and more common. This type problem could easily be given to two or more technical experts to work in their own field of technical expertise to work on the problem. Another variation of this strategy would be to simultaneously assign the problem to an expert and a nonexpert, or to a specialist and a generalist. Frequently experts and specialists get so bogged down in their own area of expertise and specialized knowledge that they overlook simple, cost-effective, and pragmatic solutions that the person with less training and predilection for the specialty would consider to be obvious. Sometimes specialists trap themselves into thinking that because a problem is complicated, or because the problem exists in a complicated area of technology, then the solution must also be complicated. Of course, this is not the case. Often the best solutions to the most complicated problems are disarmingly simple. A final variation of this strategy is designed to capitalize on people's natural tendency toward competition. The approach would be to assign the problem to two or more people, or perhaps to two or more teams of people, telling each that the assignments were being made and offering a bonus or some type of reward for the individual or group that develops the best solution. The important point to remember with all the variations of this strategy is that when all the proposals are finally completed and submitted, the manager is not obligated to use only one, or for that matter, any of them. In fact the astute manager will in all probability integrate the stronger features of each, using the stronger features to develop a final course of action that is truly synergistic.

Divide the Assignment, Giving Different Parts to Different People

This is the best course of action when the task is either too large or too complex for one person to handle alone. Since, oftentimes committee work or task-force assignments require too much coordination, this strategy has the advantage of allowing diverse talents and skills to be brought to bear on the assignment without making a great additional burden on the management of the organization. In making this type of assignment, the manager should be extremely careful to make sure each assignee fully understands: (1) exactly what is expected, and the time by which it must be completed; (2) exactly how this assignment relates to each of the other assignments, and the nature of any dependencies there might be in terms of working relationships; and (3) the big picture and how all the subparts fit together to form the big picture. If the project will encompass any length of time, it is important that intermediate checkpoints be established at the beginning to provide early warning if one or more of the assignees is encountering obstacles or delays. Many managers don't like to use this strategy because it requires a bit more coordination than most. However, if the coordination problems are anticipated and provided for in the advance planning, the process can be managed smoothly and efficiently. The key is in how much time the manager is willing to spend prior to com-

---

WHO SHOULD DO IT?
AVAILABLE CHOICES

1. ASSIGN TO THE MOST QUALIFIED PERSON.
2. ASSIGN TO ANY QUALIFIED PERSON.
3. DO IT OURSELF.
4. ASSIGN SIMULTANEOUSLY TO TWO OR MORE PEOPLE WHO WILL ACT INDEPENDENTLY.
5. DIVIDE THE ASSIGNMENT, GIVING DIFFERENT PARTS TO DIFFERENT PEOPLE.
6. ASSIGN TO A GROUP TO WORK TOGETHER.
7. DELEGATE TO WHOEVER HAS THE MOST AVAILABLE TIME.
8. ASSIGN TO ONE OR MORE PEOPLE WHO MOST NEED THE EXPERIENCE.
9. TWO OR MORE OF THE ABOVE.

FIGURE 3-1. Possible Involvement Strategies.

mencing work to make sure things happen the way they should. An additional factor to remember when employing this method is the inevitable need for joint coordination among the assignees periodically through the project. It is almost impossible for the responsible manager to provide all the coordinating necessary for a project of this size without the people working on the project occasionally meeting to discuss problems, progress, and concerns. If the project will take any reasonable amount of time (more than a few days) *brief* coordinating meetings should be scheduled for this purpose. When scheduling such a meeting make sure it is confined to coordinating activities only, and not for joint work to be completed. If the meetings turn out to be working meetings, and all the work is done during the meetings, you will have lost one of the most important benefits of this strategy. It would have been wiser to appoint a committee or task group and assign the work to them.

Assign to a Group to Work Together

This group can be called a task force, a committee, a team, or some companies, in an attempt to generate enthusiasm, have even called this kind of work group a "tiger team." Regardless of label, the important feature is that the assignment was made jointly to more than one person. This is a costly strategy in terms of work hours expended, but is justified in cases where there is a large amount of work to be done, the problem is complex, and requires people with different competencies to be able to interact with each other while working toward a solution or final decision. The demands of the situation will dictate who should participate. More will be said about how to make such selections and the criteria to use in doing so later. However, there are a few points to remember aside from these regarding the use of this strategy. When making the assignment it is imperative that, although it is a group effort, someone be in charge. Joint or dual responsibility is no responsibility. Whether you call the group a team, group, task force, or committee, it must have a leader, and the leader must be held accountable for the results and be given the authority to lead the group to the attainment of those results. It is important for the manager who is making the assignment to give as clear a definition as possible as to what the group is to achieve (i.e., what is its role and mission) and to also specify in as much detail as practical what the roles of each of the group members should be in attaining that result. Many group problem-solving activities fail for the simple reason that this charter was inadequately communicated, causing the group to get tangled up in its own processes to the extent nothing meaningful could be accomplished.

Delegate to Whoever has the most Available Time

When quality is not the primary consideration, or when expediency and urgency outweigh the concerns for quality, this could very easily be the best strategy and certainly should be given serious consideration. Once again, quality is not the foremost consideration in every single problem or decision a manager will encounter. When it's not, careful consideration should be given to balancing the workload and spreading the assignments around so everyone gets a reasonable share of the work, challenge, opportunity, satisfaction, and rewards.

Assign to One or More People who Most Need the Experience

The needs of the problem or decision itself are not the only needs a manager should consider. To some extent problems and new decisions do provide opportunities. These opportunities can take a variety of forms such as forcing new methods that are better than the old, filling people with energy and excitement as a result of being challenged, and sharpening the skills of those affected. An additional opportunity many problems provide is that they can be used to give on-the-job training with real-life problems to developing subordinates. It is one thing to learn about problem solving and decision making from a book or by participating in a training course. It is still another to watch someone else do it, and then explain what was happening and the reasons behind the decisions which were made. Although all of these learning methods are valuable and serve a useful purpose, there is nothing like doing it yourself. A great deal can be gained by giving problems to people and letting them solve the problems themselves with little help or interference from their boss. The problem though, is that most managers don't trust their subordinates enough to even let them try. They are afraid of the consequences if something should go wrong. However, if they would only stop to analyze this fear, perhaps by asking, "What's the worst thing that could happen?" they would soon realize that in most cases the fear is unrealistic and unfounded. Quite often it is possible to accomplish objectives other than those that are directly related to the problem itself. These opportunities are to be sought after and capitalized on whenever possible.

Two or More of the Above

Sometimes it will be best to think in terms of multiple strategies. For example, you may be confronted with a problem that is of pretty substantial size, which calls for a group assignment. Depending on the nature and importance of the problem, however, you might decide to make group assignments on the basis of either, (1) who in each area of expertise is most qualified; (2) who are the most available people; or (3) who needs the experience the most. Another example of a viable multiple strategy would be to divide the assignment, giving different parts to different people, but on some parts of the assigment make simultaneous assignments to two or more people.

The most important point in using any strategy is to remember to remain flexible, continuously critique progress, and to do whatever possible to use an approach and method that not only achieves the objectives of the problem or decision under consideration, but will also allow for the attainment of other objectives as well. In addition to the general guidelines presented above, there are a number of very specific factors that should be considered when deciding upon an overall strategy.

CRITERIA FOR CHOOSING OVERALL STRATEGY

The following specific factors should be assessed in order to determine the best overall strategy for a particular problem or decision.

1. *Technical or Special Knowledge Requirements.* The need to either understand the problem or develop a competent solution can frequently demand special knowledge or skills on the part of the problem solver or decision maker.

2. *Experience Requirements.* In some cases experience can prove far more valuable than the knowledge of an expert without experience. Frequently experts acquire their expertise in the laboratory or class-

room and are handicapped when it comes to being able to apply their knowledge in the less-controlled, imperfect world in which organizations actually operate. This is particularly true in the field of management where experts have found it impossible to create controlled laboratories for learning. Because of this, an experienced person with accurate recollection of past results can frequently outperform the "expert."

3. *The Need for Problem-Solving and Decision-Making Skill.* This is an important factor, because it is independent from knowledge or skill related the content of the problem. Consider the following incident. A small, high-technology company ran into difficulties with one of its highest technology products. Because of its small size, the company could not afford to maintain a full-time technical staff of great depth. At first they tried to solve the problem with available staff. Then they realized things were getting worse and the potential adverse circumstances were serious. As a result, they decided to hire an expert. So they went to the universities and recruited the best graduating Ph.D. they could find in the field. His expertise was domonstrated by his academic performance, and the work he had completed on his dissertation. He tried his best for about six months, then quit. When asked why he quit, his response was, "I went with them to solve some of their key problems, and the position sounded really challenging. But they didn't give me any real problems—all they gave me was one big mess. I never could figure out what the problem was." Of course, the problem was, in this case, that the "expert" problem solver had no problem-solving skills. Had he possessed these skills he would have been able to "sort out the mess" and approach the company's problem in a rational, logical, way that would have allowed him to bring his expertise to bear in a way that would have led to a constructive resolution of the problem. Having the specialized knowledge is not enough in itself. The problem solver must also have the ability to organize his or her efforts in such a manner that the specialized knowledge can make a true contribution.

4. *Who Will Be Affected By the Outcome?* People in management positions complain often about their frustrations in trying to overcome resistance to change. The reason a lot of people resist change is because the changes are conceived in a setting remote from these people, without their knowledge, and then are "laid on" them without an explana-

tion of how the changes were determined or the reasons they are being initiated. A lot of time can be saved in implementation, and a lot of frustration avoided, if problem solvers would determine at the outset who in the organization will be affected by the decision and include them or a representative in the process.

5. *Who Has a Stake (Gain or Loss) in the Outcome?* This is a slightly more specific consideration than the previous one. However, in taking this factor into consideration, a manager might arrive at a different list of people because of the different perspective. More consideration should be given to those who will gain or lose something than those who will be merely affected. Those who might gain something can offer support, extra resources and creative input (see Chapter 2, "Camels are O.K.," page 25). Those who have something to lose can create problems that might be avoided if they are taken into consideration when initially planning the approach. It is better to recognize the potential problem and take steps to minimize it than to ignore it for as long as possible, waiting for it to surface at some unpredictable (and most probably undesirable) time. By addressing the needs of those who are going to lose something in the involvement strategy, a lot of wasted time can usually be saved.

6. *Need for Credibility in the Process.* This is an issue far more often than might be expected. Although the people responsible for solving the problem are perfectly capable and sincere in their efforts, there may be some higher authority with whom the group has little credibility. As a result, the higher authority has little trust in the results of the group's efforts and needs some source of credibility to either validate their efforts or accept full responsibility for the recommendation. Political entities are famous for this. The city council, for example, doesn't trust the recommendation of staff (or feels that the staff recommendation would come under attack by the voting public) so they hire an outside expert to conduct a study and recommend a solution or specific course of action. This has become so common now that staffs who are frequently directed to do this type of work automatically hire a consultant even though they already know what the answer ought to be and will be. It is simply a formality to give credibility to the process.

7. *Overall Mix of Both Quality and Acceptance.*   This element could very well be the driving factor in the kind of situation where neither quality nor acceptance are of the utmost importance, but the manager is trying to get the best possible mix for both. Community planning groups are an obvious case wherein there exist a large number of special interest groups that must be appeased while at the same time both the short- and long-range best interests of the community must be satisfied. It is important, as many communities have learned from past experience, that appointments are made to such a decision-making group in such a manner that there will be enough conflict and tension between the different factions that the ultimate output from the group will be the best possible under the circumstances. In this kind of situation it is typical for people to be not completely satisfied. However, if everyone is close to being equally dissatisfied, the solution was probably the best the group could do at the time. This is an unfortunate result of human nature combined with the lack of individual problem-solving and decision-making skills of most of the people who are typically assigned to this type of group. On the quality side, although the best quality solution usually won't be the one chosen because of the necessary trade-offs for acceptance, if properly structured, the group will arrive at a solution that meets at least a minimum standard of quality in the majority of cases.

8. *The Need for Back-up Alternatives.*   This consideration could lead to the simultaneous assignment of the task to either several individuals or several groups. It could be the overriding factor in the kind of ambiguous situation where a number of different alternatives could be feasible and there is no way of determining how they will work when implemented. Typically backup alternatives should be developed when the objective is of prime importance and must be achieved without compromise. The presence of backup alternatives will substantially lower the risks involved and increase the probability of success. In comparing the weak manager to the strong one in this regard, one would find a striking difference. When confronted with an objective of absolutely essential importance, the weak manager will try to develop the very best possible approach and devote all energy and effort to seeing that the chosen alternative succeeds. The strong manager, on the other hand, is more likely in this kind of situation to assign the best people to work on a primary alternative, and simultaneously assign

other qualified people to work on additional alternatives to be implemented or partially implemented should the need arise. The strong manager does this because he or she knows that no one can predict the future. As frequently as not, some completely unforeseen event or set of circumstances will present itself, causing the "best" alternative to look ludicrous at worst and inappropriate at best.

9. *The Need for Diversity in Approaches.* Aligned with the need for backup alternatives is the need for diversity in approaches. Although some people argue that a manager should always strive for a wide diversity in approaches, it is probably much more practical to operate on the assumption that some situations will be affected more than others by this factor. When the need is present, simultaneous or divided assignments will probably contribute most to satisfying the need.

10. *The Need to Minimize Possible Adverse Personal Consequences.* Often referred to as "PMA," this factor is often overlooked or disregarded as a legitimate concern when formulating problem-solving and decision-making strategies. It should not be. Although this should never be the overriding factor, it should always be considered. If a manager is competent and capable, then that manager has a responsibility to the company as well as to self to ensure that today's actions do not lead to adverse personal consequences that could either threaten the manager's career or his/her relationship with the company. When risk is assessed, it should be assessed from both the perspective of the company and of the individual manager.

11. *Political Requirements (Internal and External).* Political requirements here means the practical considerations related to the needs of competing interest groups or individuals, particularly those who are in, or are competing for, positions of leadership, power, or influence. These individuals or groups could be either internal to the organization or external. In the private sector, the external political considerations are becoming so abundant as to be almost overpowering. Whether this is right or wrong, it is virtual suicide to ignore this reality when taking management action. An example of the embarrassment that can result from ignoring political considerations is what happened to the operating division of a major Midwest energy company when the top management of the division decided to move their headquarters from a

small town in the Midwest to Chicago. The division's business involved travel all over the Midwest as well as having people from all over the Midwest travel to headquarters. Transportation services in and out of the headquarters town were poor. In addition, it was difficult to recruit and maintain staff in all the required areas. These and many other problems could be solved by moving the headquarters. No one could think of any major business reasons why the division should not move to Chicago. So the decision was made and all the plans were put into action. However, on the day of the move, the Chairman of the Board of the parent company read about it in the morning paper. This was the first he had heard about it. The move was contrary to promises he had previously made to community leaders about maintaining a good base of operations, and thus supporting the local economy, in their community. The Chairman immediately phoned the head of the division and canceled the move. The confusion, frustration, and costs that resulted were tremendous. All of these could have been avoided had the responsible managers been sensitive to the political requirements of the situation or at least developed a strategy that would allow them to surface.

12. *Who Can Benefit From This Assignment?*   An ongoing responsibility of every manager is to develop subordinates to the highest level of proficiency possible. Career needs, developmental needs, and individual aspirations of subordinates should be taken into account at every possible level. Frequently the person who needs it the most will also do the best job, regardless of comparative measures of competence, skill level, and expertise at the outset.

Each of these factors should be considered for every new problem or decision, while recognizing that the relative level of importance for each will vary with the circumstances. Another way of considering those dimensions that are most important is to develop the habit of asking the following four questions before beginning work on the task.

1. Who should be involved in the process?
2. Who should be consulted before the final decision?
3. Who shuld be informed afterward?
4. Who should be responsible for managing the process?

Frequent and repeated use of these questions will help to put the issues of overall strategy in perspective. They should be used, as should all the factors mentioned be considered, before proceeding with the actual problem-solving and decision-making activities outlined by the Lyles Method. But after having considered all these factors, the choices regarding strategy will not have been completely dispensed with. For at each stage of activity there are choices to make regarding what is the best possible method to approach the situation in order to arrive at the best possible course of action.

These substrategies, or process strategies as they are called, are presented in detail in the following seven chapters. They too, must be practiced and mastered in order to attain true problem-solving and decision-making proficiency.

Part II
Seven Steps to Practical Problem Solving and Decision Making for Managers

4
Defining the Problem

The importance of defining a problem has been stated a number of ways. However none has probably been more forceful or accurate than the following statement of Albert Einstein. He said,

> The formulation of a problem is far more often essential than its solution, which may be merely a matter of mathematical or experimental skill.

If a problem is not clearly understood, then the likelihood of a chosen solution being successful is much less than if the problem is clearly understood. When the problem is not understood, you are at best firing blind, hoping your solutions will have some effect. When the problem is understood the definition becomes a target—a focal point toward which to channel your problem-solving activities.

Problems are one of two things. Either they are, (1) obstacles, conditions, or phenomena which *stand in the way* of achieving desired objectives; or (2) they are obstacles, conditions, or phenomena which *are causing a deviation* from the desired status. The common characteristic of both is that they describe undesirable factors that must be dealt with if the desired organizational results are to be achieved. These factors can be either human, operational, or technical in nature. Because of their undesirability they must be dealt with. They must be either eliminated, circumnavigated, or their adverse effects minimized or neutralized. In order to do any of these, however, the problems must first be understood.

Defining the problem means to *identify and describe* the obstacles, conditions, or phenomena which stand in the way of achieving objectives or are causing a deviation from the desired status. Problems exist when something is wrong. A problem is well defined when the manager understands what is wrong with enough comprehension to be able to tell others about the situation in terms they can understand *and* to be able to generate possible solutions that will eliminate the problem.

There is a big difference between being able to know something is wrong and to generally describe some of the more obvious characteristics, and being able to demonstrate understanding on a deep enough level so the true causes of a problem can be dealt with. Examination of the following case will help to illustrate this difference. This case was presented by a supervisor exactly as follows:

> During the past three months an engineer I supervise has begun to exhibit substandard performance in both quantity and quality of work. In addition, his job attendance has been less than satisfactory. He leaves early at the end of the day and just about every Friday afternoon comes up with some excuse to leave, such as having a doctor's appointment, he has relatives arriving at the airport on an early flight, etc.
>
> This engineer has been employed by the company for about two years and would be hard (if not impossible) to replace promptly. He has been told on several occasions that his work is not up to standard, and he has promised to improve. But as of yet this has not happened. What can I do?

This is not an uncommon problem. The same situation, with only minor variations occurs quite frequently. However, it is not a problem that gets solved satisfactorily very often. The reason is that most managers and supervisors, when confronted with it, give only a cursory analysis, immediately implementing a solution that does not adequately address the true problem.

Most managers, when asked what to do about this problem, say, "Well, it's fairly obvious. The guy is not doing his job. You'd better talk to him, may be in a formal counseling session, tell him what you think of his performance, and let him know that if it doesn't improve, you're going to have to let him go." This is the most typical response, and probably the worst possible way to address the problem.

The first consideration is that the supervisor in the case has already done this and it isn't working. The second factor is that the suggested approach doesn't address the critical dynamic that is occurring here. The engineer worked well for twenty-one months of employment. Only during the last three months has his performance deteriorated. For whatever reason, he has lost interest in his work. It could be that other outside interests have taken over, diverting his energies and attention elsewhere; it could be that he has simply become bored with his work; or it could be that he has become aware that he does not see a long-range career path or future in his current situation. It is the manager's responsibility to find out which of these is the case. Only when this has been accomplished is it safe to say the problem has been defined.

When a particular solution or course of action does not produce the desired result, it is probably because the solution does not deal with the true problem. In talking to the engineer, the supervisor must have been missing something, or the behavior would have improved. Of course, the key element missing in the supervisor's definition of the problem was the engineer's loss of interest in his work. This led to an inadequate solution and a lack of resolution of the problem.

TWO PRINCIPLES FOR DEFINING PROBLEMS

Problem-defining activities should always take into account two fundamental concepts regarding the nature of problems. First is that problems arise only in the context of accomplishment, and second is that when a problem occurs, it occurs because something caused it to occur. Let's examine the context issue first.

The Context of Accomplishment

In Chapter 1 it was pointed out that management activity starts out with a decision to accomplish something. Whether implicit or explicit, operating organizations have some kind of hierarchy of purpose (i.e., mission, goals, and objectives) that each organization is trying to accomplish. A problem occurs and becomes a problem then in one of two ways. The first way is when obstacles, events, or phenomena arise that stand in the way of achieving this already-defined hierarchy of purpose. The second is when a deviation occurs that causes events to swerve from an already-established level of functioning. Conditions, events, or phenomena *cannot* be classified as problems unless they are preventing the attainment of desired objectives or are causing deviations from a desired level of performance. This is why we say that problems arise only in the context of accomplishments.

To better understand what this means, a diagram might be helpful. In the diagram let's call these accomplishments Desired Results (DR). We must assume that these results are on a different level than any results that existed previously and that it will take a significant amount of time to produce the Desired Results. If the results aren't significant or the time required to produce them substantial, there is no need for an organization to begin with. We must also assume that the activity started at some point where the results that were then being produced were different from the Desired Results which led to the formation of the organization. The diagram looks like this:

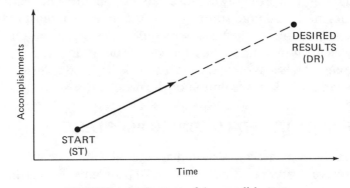

FIGURE 4–1. Context of Accomplishment.

The scale at the left gives an indication of different levels of accomplishment. The scale across the bottom represents time. The Start point is representative of the organization's beginning situation, and the Desired Results point indicates the level of accomplishment the organization is striving for. The vector connecting the Start and Desired Results points represents the activity that is taking place as the organization tries to accomplish its Desired Results.

A problem then, is something that disrupts this activity. It is either an obstacle that prevents further desired activity or an event or condition that causes some other results to occur. A problem might be depicted on the graph on one of several ways depending upon the effect it created. If it is merely an obstacle to further progress, it would be shown as follows:

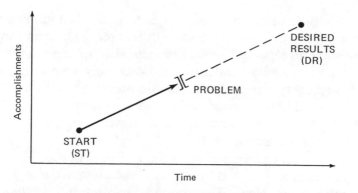

FIGURE 4–2. Problem as Obstacle.

If it is causing activities to be thrown off course, so that different results are being produced, it might be shown in one of the following ways, depending on the effect the problem has on accomplishments relative to time.

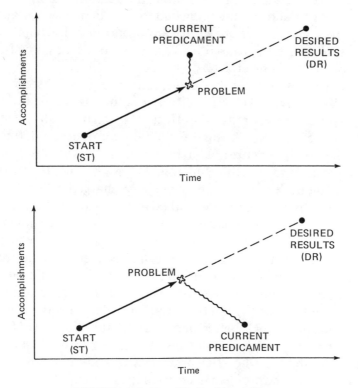

FIGURE 4–3. Possible Problem Effects.

Now it should be relatively easy to understand the logic behind the statement that problems only exist in the context of accomplishment. If there were no Desired Results to begin with, then no matter what happened, there would be no problem. Something is a problem only if it stands in the way of the achievement of a previously specified Desired Result. Accordingly, a good definition will speak to this Desired Result. It will explicitly address the context of accomplishment in which the problem exists.

There are other elements of a good problem definition, but before examining them let's look at the second fundamental concept regarding the nature of problems. The second principle deals with the logic of cause and effect.

The Logic of Cause and Effect

Logic tells us that when something happens, there is usually a specific cause that made it happen. For example, if a person is riding down the road and gets a flat tire, something had to have happened to cause the tire to go flat. The same can be said of any occurrence. If it happened, it was because something caused it to happen—there was a cause or a reason for the resulting effect.

Focusing on cause rather than effect can make a big difference in the final results achieved. The most effective solutions will be those that deal with the cause rather than the effect. This can be vividly illustrated in the flat tire example. Assume for a moment that you defined the problem in terms of the tire not having any air in it. An unlikely definition in a problem such as this, but nonetheless possible. If you knew a little more about the circumstances but were charged with solving the problem, an obvious solution would be to fill the tire with air. Unless there is a gaping and obvious hole, the tire is then likely to hold the air adequately until you've been on the road again for awhile at which time it will go flat again. You will not have dealt effectively with the problem in this case because of your focus on the effect and not the cause.

On the other hand, had you observed the flat tire, realized that something had caused the tire to go flat, and identified the cause, the result would be a much better definition of the problem. Not only would it be more precise, it would also be more helpful. Assume for a moment that the tire when flat because it picked up a nail from the road. By defining the problem in terms of the hole and the nail, a much different set of solutions is likely to be developed. The difference now is that the solutions will be much more effective in permanently dealing with the "problem." The definition will cause the problem activities to focus on the nail and the hole as well as the lack of air, thus causing a much more viable result to be accomplished.

The flat tire example very vividly illustrates the concept of cause and effect related to problems. Unfortunately, most management problems are more ambiguous and the cause and effect relationships are usually much more difficult to identify and address. Consider again the example of the engineer mentioned earlier in the chapter. If the manager's confrontation addresses only the incidents of leaving early and substandard work performance on an incident-by-incident basis, a lasting solution is unlikely. This would be like pumping air into the flat tire. On the other hand, if the manager probes beneath the surface, a much more meaningful definition of the problem is likely to be developed. The observable behaviors are really effects resulting from some underlying cause. In this case the cause of these behaviors was that the engineer had lost interest in his work. He no longer felt any of the challenge, excitement, or enthusiasm he experienced during the first couple of years on the job. A lasting and practical solution to the problem must take this into account. Anything else would only work for the short run because it would address only the effects and not the true cause.

In looking at the diagram of problems then, another important facet of problem definitions can be illustrated. It is important that the definition take into account the cause, that is the specific events, conditions, or phenomena, that made things go awry. It is also important to know where things currently stand in relation to the desired results. But what is in between—the effects or symptoms—are of secondary importance.

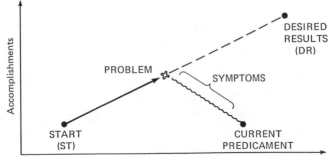

Now we have all the ingredients necessary for a sufficient problem definition: (1) A context of accomplishment; (2) the relationship of current predicament to desired results; and (3) focus on the cause of the undesired effects. However before examining the different strategies used to develop problem definitions there are certain characteristics associated with different kinds of problems that should be understood.

FACTORS TO CONSIDER WHEN DEFINING DIFFERENT KINDS OF PROBLEMS

In Chapter 1 three categories of problems were presented: People, Operational, and Technical. People problems are those problems that are caused primarily by the actions of individuals or groups that are, for all practical purposes, unique to the people involved. Operational problems, although they may involve people, are caused by factors other than human initiative. They are problems of organization, marketing, regulation, policy, finance, and so on. Technical problems are those stemming from mechanical, electrical, electronic, hydraulic, component, and/or system malfunctioning. A review of some of the examples presented on pages 11 to 21 in Chapter 1 might be helpful at this point to refresh your memory as to the characteristics of typical problems in each category. In addition to the distinctions addressed in Chapter 1, several other factors should be understood as an aid to problem definition activities.

NATURE OF AVAILABLE INFORMATION

The first factor to consider is the kind of information or data the manager will have to work with when attacking the different kinds of problems. Technical problems will usually lend themselves to very specific, concrete definitions. The data used in analysis will almost always be quantifiable and straightforward, including such things as production quantities, yield statistics, volumes, down-time statistics, or failure rates, to name a few. People problems, on the other hand, are usually couched in vague, somewhat more ambiguous terms, shaded by different perceptions and made unclear by different interpretations. Operational problems fall somewhere in between. These graduations of clarity can be shown on a continuum as follows:

People	TYPE OF PROBLEM Operational	Technical
Vague		Precise
Ambiguous		Detailed
Obscure		Specific

CLARITY OF DATA

The reason it is important to note these differences is that they dictate a different demand for rigor in defining each type of problem. When the data is clear and precise, as with technical problems, then the utmost should be demanded in determining specifically what cause is producing the undesired effect. The solution then becomes almost obvious and one is likely to achieve near-perfect results. At the other extreme, when true cause may be much more difficult to ascertain, to be rigorous in pursuing certain proof of cause could mean being irresponsibly unproductive.

When we hear people say managers need to develop a greater tolerance for ambiguity, this factor is most probably what they are alluding to, since the majority of problems managers face on a routine basis are operational and people oriented. Frustration results when they find they are unable to "gather all the facts" adequately enough to create a crisp, clear, cut-and-dried picture of the problem. Engineers-turned-manager are especially vulnerable to this frustration. Having launched their careers working on engineering problems, where there is always a specific, data-based explanation, their frustration level soars when confronted with the mainstream of management problems where the "facts" are always preceded by qualifiers like maybe, could be, and probably. However, let me hasten to add, this is not a derogatory evaluation of the thought processes of engineers. My experience has been that engineers who successfully make the adjustment to higher tolerances for ambiguity typically make better managers than those without previous technical backgrounds. Although I am not aware of any research in this area, I am willing to venture a hypothesis that this results from them having first developed the fairly rigorous thought processes required to accomplish technical work.

THE NATURE OF THE CAUSE-AND-EFFECT RELATIONSHIP

The second factor that varies among the different kinds of problems is the nature and clarity of the cause-and-effect relationship. For every effect or set of effects there is a cause. Technical problems are usually the result of a single event or condition. When there is more than one undesirable cause in technical situations gone awry, these multiple causes usually appear in a series or sequence. This allows the problem solver the opportunity to follow a fairly logical progression backward to the event or condition that triggered the first set of undesirable effects. Persistence and logic will almost always lead to a satisfactory explanation of the circumstances. This is not necessarily the case with operational and people problems.

Both people and operational problems have a human behavior component to them. People problems are so labeled because they result from human initiative at the causal level. Although difference causes are the source of operating problems, people become involved in the process at either the intervening or output level in order for there to be a problem. Thus, to one extent or the other, people are involved in shaping the dynamics of both kinds of problems. It is an understatement to say that human beings and human behavior are complex. Although we are learning more every day, the reasons (i.e, causes) people act the way they do most of the time are still not very clearly understood. Because the causes of human behavior are for the most part unknown, defining causes in problems with human behavior components can be difficult.

Many managers, however, feel they must "prove" cause before accepting a definition for a problem in these areas. Attempting this can be a waste of time. Organizations are not courts of law and management is not a formal judiciary process. There is a certain amount of risk that is necessary for a manager to accomplish meaningful results. A good part of this risk is felt when circumstances dictate that action must be taken in spite of the fact that there is no way of completely eliminating uncertainty.

ASSUMPTIONS CONSTRUED AS FACT

A third factor, although sometimes having an effect in all types of problems, most frequently affects the understanding of operational problems. It has to do with people construing assumptions pertaining to external events as fact. In Chapter 2 a number of ideas regarding the relationship between facts and assumptions were presented. Here we move from the general to a more specific type of situation where misunderstandings in this area can cause serious negative consequences. No one really knows why, but quite often people's assumptions regarding external events get construed as fact. Irving Janis, in some of his research in the area of Groupthink, says one possible cause for this could be that members of a group have a natural need to create a "we-they" attitude between themselves and those outside the group (or organization). This, coupled with another common group tendency to want to sound rational and objective, could unconsciously create a tendency to give a "factual" aura to circumstances the group is not in direct contact with. A greater feeling (although a false feeling) of security is thus generated that the actions of the group are well grounded. Of course it is also much easier and more expeditious over the short run to simply treat assumptions as facts than to carry out the investigative work necessary to verify their validity.

INTERRELATIONSHIP OF DATA

A fourth factor deals with the interrelationships of data. Data are irrelevant unless a specific relationship to a problem can be delineated. Data reported under one set of circumstances, or in groupings with other data might imply one interpretation. Reported with another set of data they might imply no problem at all or a completely different interpretation. When defining problems take care that the data upon which you base your findings are interpreted in the proper context. More important, be alert to whatever interrelationships between data may exist.

STRATEGIES FOR DEFINING PROBLEMS

The four most common strategies for defining problems are: (1) Describe, (2) Differentiate, (3) Reconstruct, and (4) Separate. Here is what each means along with some guidance on how they can best be applied.

Describe

The describe strategy is to give a detailed account of the problem in words (either verbally or in writing) so as to present a thorough description of the cause of the problem and its effect on the manager's area of responsibility. As presented earlier, the description should explain the situation thoroughly enough so that all conclusions regarding causality and the effect on end results can be thoroughly understood. All significant factors, including any necessary historical data of future implications should be included in the description.

The final description of the problem should consist of two levels of explanation. The first level is the nature of the problem and its effect. The second is any additional data needed to fully understand the dynamics of the problem. The most practical way to approach the first level is to use a standard format. Since problems are one of two things (either obstacles or deviations), one of two simple formats should suffice for the problem statement. Figure 4-4 shows both formats. The first example would be used in the case where an obstacle was preventing the accomplishment of already established goals. The second would be used in the case where something was causing undesired effects to occur.

Format #1:   (A very specific causal condition, event, or phenomena)   , is preventing   (very specific desired results)   , from happening.

Format #2:   (A very specific causal condition, event, or phenomena)   , is causing   (very specific UNdesired results , to occur.

FIGURE 4-4. Format For Problem Definition Statements.

Once the problem statement is formulated, a decision should be made as to whether or not additional information is needed in order to fully understand the problem.

For example, refer to the problem regarding the engineer that was presented at the beginning of this chapter. The strategy of Describe is the most efficient strategy to use for this and similar type problems. Describe is probably always the best strategy to use when there is a lack of clear-cut data (by clear-cut here we mean quantifiable and specific) to give a true picture of causality. The first decision that needs to be made is whether the problem falls into the obstacle or the deviation category. There is no evidence that his performance is standing in the way of any significant accomplishments. However, the report does indicate that he performed satisfactorily for the first twenty-one of the past twenty-four months. Since we had a satisfactory performance that has now deteriorated into unsatisfactory performance, it is safe to conclude that this problem belongs in the deviation category. Thus we will use Format #2 from Figure 4-4. To do so we will have to specify a causal condition and an undesirable set of effects. Let's look at the causal condition component first.

It is insufficient to repeat the events that have already been reported as part of the problem definition. There is no value whatsoever in repeating the fact that he has poor attendance, leaves early, and the quality of his work is declining. What is most important is the cause of these events. Many managers, when given this problem, either focus on the reported events as the problem, or say they need more information to define the problem well enough to be able to act on it. Both are wrong. By examining the data in its entirety, there is a realistic and accurate conclusion that can be drawn from this report that will lead to an adequate solution to the problem. Looking at the entire report, what conclusions can you arrive at regarding the basic cause of the engineer's behavior?

Can you say the engineer is acting the way he is because he is an alcoholic? Although some alcoholics behave in ways that are very similar to the engineer, this would not be a valid conclusion. It may be part of the problem, but we have no way of knowing from the data that it is present. It's unlikely in this case, because usually when alcoholism is the problem, there is evidence to indicate its presence. Maybe he has developed a romantic involvement away from work that is interfering with his ability to concentrate. But if that's the case, is the problem capable of being dealt with by the supervisor on that level? Not properly. Lots of other possibilities exist that simply don't fit the data. Maybe he's moonlighting or getting involved in local politics. We could go on forever speculating on this rather nonproductive level of specificity to no avail. But what can we safely say? We can safely say that he has lost interest in his work, for whatever reason. This is the one explanation that fits all the data. Nothing else fits the report or the circumstances. Anything less specific will not suffice in leading to an adequate resolution of the problem. Failure to take the loss of interest into account is probably what caused the previous attempts at solving the problem to fail. To warn him about his poor performance without addressing the interest loss is almost sure to guarantee failure.

Now let's examine the second segment of the format. The task here is to describe the specific undesired results that are being caused. It is sufficient here to go with the obvious and state that his behavior is causing his work performance to deteriorate to unacceptable levels. This is the reason his behavior is a problem.

The problem statement could be written as follows:

"The engineer has lost interest in his work, causing his performance on the job to drop below acceptable levels."

Using this definition as the foundation for problem-solving activities will provide a higher probability of success than any other definition. If it turns out that during the course of problem-solving activities more specific data is revealed as to why he is losing interest, then the working definition would be revised and the direction of problem-solving activity adjusted to account for the new information. The point is, with this definition you won't miss the target. You may narrow the focus from time to time, but you'll always be heading in the right direction.

Now we should take into account the second level of explanation. The first level, as we have seen, details cause and effect. The second level provides any necessary additional data that helps to explain conditions in a way that will provide greater understanding. If you were the engineer's supervisor in this case and were going to solve the problem yourself, the second level would not be required. However, if the engineer permanently worked in another department and was on temporary assignment to you, it might be appropriate to notify his permanent supervisor or department head of the problem. In this situation it might be of great help to add a brief explanatory paragraph describing his actions that led you to the conclusion.

In summary, the first level of description should always be used. One of the two formats presented in Figure 4–4 should be followed, depending on whether the problem fits the category of obstacle or deviation. In cases where a deeper level of understanding is necessary, the second level of description should be provided. This consists of a brief supporting paragraph presenting whatever additional information will contribute to a more meaningful understanding of the problem.

DIFFERENTIATE

The strategy of Differentiate (sometimes referred to as Distinguish) calls for defining the problem by comparing situations that are producing the desired result with those that aren't to find the exact cause of the discrepancy. Differentiating is probing to uncover what is different in one set of circumstances from one or more different set of circumstances that is causing a problem.

Obviously, differentiate requires a comparative data base to work. The problem situation has to have features that have occurred in the historical situation.

Most of the problems that lend themselves to this kind of analysis are of the deviation type rather than the obstacle type. However, the major determining factor in deciding to use the strategy of Differentiate is whether or not a comparative data base exists. Once the determination has been made that a comparative data base (either historical or concurrent) exists, the following procedure should be followed to define the problem:

1. *Determine the Nature of the Data Base and the Outside Parameters of Interest.* What kind of data is relevant? Which areas are adversely affected and which are not? What is the extent of the problem? How long has the problem been a problem? Who is involved? What geographical boundaries describe the problem?

2. *Identify all the Differences Between What is Working (or What Has Worked In the Past) From What is Not Working.* Are the materials, operators, set-ups, tests, monitoring mechanisms, and processes the same? What differences exist in equipment? Are the qualifications of the people involved different? What else is different? What about maintenance procedures?

3. *Determine Which Differences are Causing the Problem.* If something different is happening, something else has to be causing it. What is it? Is there more than one cause? Can you verify for certain which difference is causing the undesired effect?

Upon completion of these three steps the problem should be clearly defined. Your definition should then be able to be translated into the format for problem definitions presented under the Describe strategy on page 82, Figure 4-4.

RECONSTRUCT

To reconstruct is to recreate, to the best of one's ability, either with words, pictures, other visual aids (such as models or charts), or actual residue, a problem situation or crisis that occurred previously. Reconstruct offers most help to the kinds of problems that are major in scope (disasters, for example) and need to be understood so that similar problems can be avoided in the future. Some technical problems fall into this category, as do some operational problems. Very few people problems are such that the Reconstruct strategy offers much help in defining the problem. In the Engineer problem example at the beginning of this chapter, for example, Reconstruct might help some in better understanding the interrelationships between events, but probably not any more so than the method recommended.

An example of a type of problem that could best be approached using this strategy is an airline crash. The breakdown of the nuclear reactor plant at Three Mile Island is another. In both cases there is little that can be accomplished in terms of the problem that has already occurred. However, it is of utmost importance that everything that happened be fully understood in order that steps can be taken to prevent similar disasters in the future.

Like the strategy of Differentiate, the Reconstruct strategy relies heavily on data or evidence to provide understanding. Good data-gathering techniques and observational abilities are prerequisites to success with this strategy. The sections on "Asking the Right Questions" and on "Developing the Ability to Reconstruct Remote Events" in Chapter 2 are especially pertinent to the use of this strategy.

Because this strategy tends to focus back in time on events that have already occurred, it carries with it the possibility that certain portions of important data may be lost or forgotten. Once something has vanished, it is extremely difficult to verify its past existence. For this reason it is important that the problem solver always bear in mind the consideration that additional circumstances may have existed at one time and left no traces. An additional factor associated with hindsight is the confusion that often arises between facts and assumptions. As pointed out earlier, this can always be a problem. However, when recalling events from the past, it presents a very special problem, because of the human mind's tendency to confuse the two when recalling past events. If a person makes an assumption in real time, they are usually aware they are making an assumption. If however, they perceive something, assume an explanation for that perceived experience, file the perception away in their memory banks, and then recall it at some future time, they are likely to recall the perception as fact. If the assumed explanation for what they perceived was erroneous, then what they later perceive to be fact will also be erroneous. However, the recollection will cause more problems because the person won't be aware that there was an assumption involved in the perceptual process at one point in time.

Upon completion of the reconstruction process, once again the definition of the problem should lend itself to one of our problem definition formats. This should always be the final test of problem definition activities. If the definition fits one of the formats in Figure 4-4, then it is most probably an adequate definition. Since reconstruct will most likely be used in deviation type problems, format #2 is the one that will probably be used most often to present the definition achieved through the reconstruct strategy.

SEPARATE

The strategy of Separate is used to divide complex problems into smaller analytical frameworks, or to divide the responsibilities in a particularly complex situation into more manageable components so the smaller issues can be fully understood before attempting to solve the entire problem as a whole.

Operational problems typically lend themselves more to the use of the strategy of Separate than do most people or technical problems, although it is possible to think of examples of all three types that would fit. An example of the type of problem that would best be approached using this strategy would be the following. For the past six months the company has been losing sales. Earnings and cash flow are down, and morale is low. On the surface, this problem looks as though it has a simple and straightforward definition related to the sagging sales. However, a more experienced manager would be quick to point out that there is no way this problem could be that simple. A number of different factors are probably contributing to the decline. But that is not all that needs to be considered here. What about the effects of reduced cash flow on production? And what about the morale issue? Is it serious enough to cause things to get even worse?

Depending on the particular circumstances of this situation a number of separate problems should be analyzed in detail. The sales problem, of course needs to be addressed directly. But more understanding is likely to be gained sooner if it is divided into several categories of analysis. For example, could the cause be problems with the quality of the product? Has increased activity from competitors caused a loss of some of the market share? Have financial conditions in the economy shifted in a way that precludes purchase of the product? Depending upon the manager's sense of which of the factors may be exerting a dominant influence on events, priorities for analysis can be established and problem definition activities can be delegated to experts in the different areas. Then someone else should start working on the impact of reduced cash flow on the company. Perhaps the manufacturing and finance people need to work jointly. The personnel department should probably be involved in trying to define the morale problem and the extent its effect might have in the future.

Once again, the final test of the definition should be whether it can fit in the problem definition format. When the strategy of separate is used (often in conjunction with other strategies), instead of finishing the process with only one statement, it is very likely that there could be a half-dozen or more problem statements. Each one of the problem statements then serves as a starting point for carrying out the remaining six steps of the Lyles Method.

5
Defining Objectives

Good management is nothing more than common sense applied. The problem is that common sense changes daily. The common sense of yesterday is no longer valid in many areas of management today. And because it changes so often in so many areas of management responsibility, what was common sense yesterday simply cannot be taken for granted today. Consider for example, the area of personnel practices. Equal opportunity laws and regulations have made what many managers in the past considered to be "common sense" in hiring practices, firing practices, promotional procedures, and treatment of employees in general, to be considered obsolete foolishness today. Safety is another area where the changes in what a manager can consider "common sense" have been dramatic. OSHA Regulations and court rulings have had a profound effect on our most basic attitudes and philosophies regarding management and supervision. But government regulation isn't the only force causing our attitudes and understanding to change. The ever dynamic forces in the marketplace, changing consumer attitudes, shifting values in society and the workforce, and the steady stream of improvements in technology, all contribute to changes in what the common sense of management for any given moment ought to be.

Because of this, the *objectives* of management ought to be under constant scrutiny to determine if they are still valid in light of the new circumstances of the day. In other words, one must assume the circumstances will change to keep pace only if the responsible members of management take affirmative action to make them change. New information and new circumstances will drive the need for new objectives and new directions. Although this will not always be the case, it will be true in enough situations to warrant a review and reassessment of those objectives affected by problems and decisions when those problems and decisions are confronted.

The objectives of management and the overall goals of the organization should not change with every passing problem or decision. However, it is critically important that each manager know exactly how the solution to every problem and the result of each decision relate to the organization's hierarchy of objectives. The two must be compatible. Every planned action should fit with the total scheme of things.

Thus, when solving problems and making decisions, objectives should be defined on two levels. First the manager should define the overall objective—what are the key results to be achieved in this area of management responsibility. And second, what are the objectives of this particular management action. A large number of needless problems could be avoided if responsible managers would take at least a short time to review objectives in light of the circumstances of the day rather than rush to the solution without using objectives to guide them. Consider the following true case.

A number of years ago a small town outside Paris, France, had a problem with their fire department. Like many small towns, this particular city couldn't afford to hire a full-time staff of fire fighters. Because of the town's size, the citizens had to rely on volunteers. When the town was small, this proved to be a practical approach. The city was able to maintain a very dedicated group of volunteers who derived great satisfaction from their efforts and enjoyed the excitement and feelings of accomplishment the work provided. As the town grew, however, the burden on the volunteers increased as well. After a while the load became especially heavy as fire-fighting duties began to interfere quite substantially with family and social life and responsibilities at work.

It wasn't long before the volunteers went before the Town Council and registered their complaints. They explained that although they were happy to do the work, it was becoming an ever-increasing burden on them personally. They asked if the Council couldn't do something to alleviate the burden. The Council responded favorably, expressing their appreciation for the dedicated service. After reviewing the matter, however, they found that although the tax coffers had increased in size with the growth of the town, there were still insufficient funds to be able to afford a full-time fire-fighting staff. Since both the council and the fire-fighters were eager to find a solution to the problem, they appointed a committee comprised of fire-fighters, council members, and concerned citizens to solve the problem.

The problem-solving committee met for several weeks before finally arriving at a solution everyone was excited about. The solution was a relatively simple one. Since there was not enough money to provide full-time salaries, the committee proposed that a reimbursement system be established whereby the fire fighters would be paid for the fires they put out. This seemed especially fair, since if there were fewer fires, the imposition on the fire fighters would be smaller and thus the town could save money. When there were more fires, the town would be receiving a higher level of service, the fire fighters would be making greater sacrifices, and thus the town should be willing to pay more. They implemented the plan with optimism.

Several months later the local gendarmes were called out in the middle of the night on a tip that a group of thugs were digging up the railway tracks on the Paris express line just outside town. The law-enforcement officials nabbed the thugs in the act, loaded them into the paddy wagon and headed for jail. During the trip, however, one of the gendarmes noticed a look of familiarity among the thugs. He suddenly turned and asked, "Hey, aren't you fellows members of our local fire department?" When they sheepishly responded in the affirmative they were then asked what they were doing. They answered, "We only get paid for the emergencies we respond to, and we thought we could be really helpful in a big one!" Subsequent investigations revealed they had been dashing all about the countryside for the past few months lighting fires. Then they would hurry home and respond to the emergency so they could chalk up another paycheck.

What seemed at first to be a logical and fair solution to the compensation problem at the French fire department backfired because everyone failed to first take into account the overall objective of the town and its citizenry. This is a classic case of problem solving without first establishing a common and clear-cut vision of the total results and final outcomes desired from the organization. The problem solvers performed fairly well in achieving the second-level objectives—to find a way to compensate the fire fighters. But they missed the overall objectives of the fire department completely—to protect the citizens and their property from the ravages of fire. The chosen solution took them in exactly the opposite direction.

The events at the French fire department did not occur just because the people involved were French or the employees were fire fighters. Less interesting versions of this story unfold daily around the world in all kinds of organizations because managers are too eager to solve problems—that is, come up with a solution—without first determining how everything fits together from top to bottom. The costs of failing to take the time to determine how a particular problem relates to all other facets of an organization's operations are substantial. This is the one short cut that always turns out to be the long cut in the long run.

> WHEN DEFINING OBJECTIVES, IT IS IMPORTANT TO DO SO ON TWO LEVELS: FIRST IS THE OVERALL LEVEL IN THAT ORGANIZATION'S AREA OF RESPONSIBILITY; SECOND IS THE LEVEL OF THE SPECIFIC OBJECTIVES OF THE PROBLEM OR DECISION UNDER CONSIDERATION.

To better understand this concept it is helpful to refer back to the diagram used in the previous chapter, showing the relationship between problems, desired results, and accomplishments. It is reproduced here for each reference.

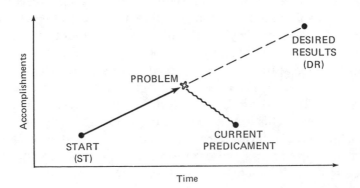

Once the problem has been defined and the current predicament (and its cause) are fully understood, we now concentrate on setting objectives. A number of options exist, the most obvious of which include:

1. Trying to go from where we are now to the Desired Results that were initially defined.
2. Restoring circumstances to the point at which they departed from the original path, then proceeding toward the initial Desired Results.
3. Changing the overall objectives and proceeding to try to accomplish a completely new set of Desired Results.
4. Abandoning this set of Desired Results completely and dedicating our resources elsewhere.

Each of these options would be depicted on our diagram in the following manner:

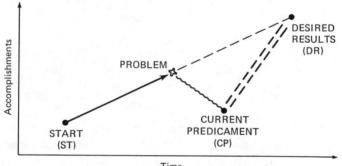

FIGURE 5-1. Objective from CP to DR.

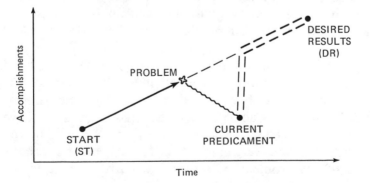

FIGURE 5-2. Objective to Restore Then Go To DR.

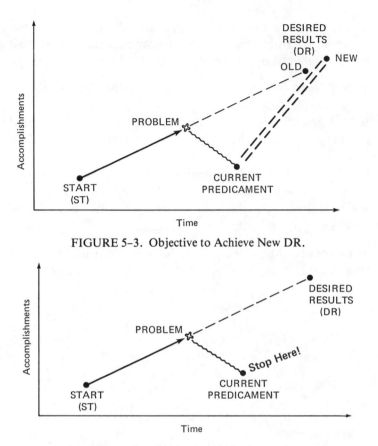

FIGURE 5–3. Objective to Achieve New DR.

FIGURE 5–4. Objective from CP to DR.

Although these options have been defined in terms of problem-solving situations, the same basic precepts apply in decision-making situations where no current problems exist. When the Lyles Method is used for decision making only, in the absence of apparent problems, then the object defining step is the place to start. Decision making for managers means choosing which activities will be carried out by the organization and how they will be carried out. Thus the proper place to start decision-making activities is with management's objectives. The relationship between the various factors involved would be very similar, and the diagrams very much alike. The only differences will be the absence of any problem indicators. The current situation would be shown as follows:

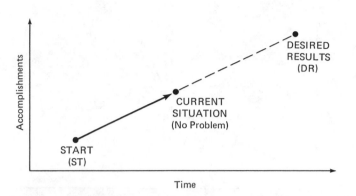

FIGURE 5-5. Things Proceeding on Track.

This diagram shows things are on track—proceeding on schedule toward accomplishment of the desired results. If the manager here is alert, then he or she will be periodically reviewing objectives and the approach used to achieve them, and also will be searching for new accomplishments to pursue and potential problems to avoid. More explicitly stated, the options include:

1. Building on existing strengths to improve the overall level of accomplishment.
2. Seeking new opportunities to exploit—to pursue new and different accomplishments.
3. Avoiding potential problems that might arise in the future to prevent accomplishment of the desired results.

Each of these options can be diagrammed as follows:

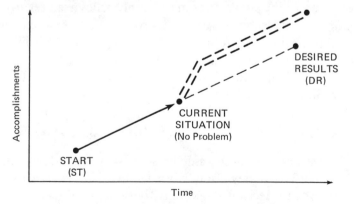

FIGURE 5-6. Improving Level of Accomplishment.

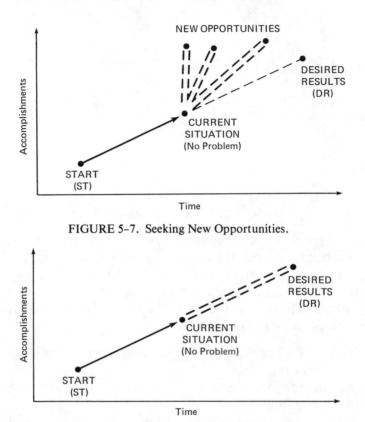

FIGURE 5-7. Seeking New Opportunities.

FIGURE 5-8. Avoiding Future Problems.

In comparing the methods for developing objectives then, we see that there are striking similarities in the approaches used regardless of whether or not there is the presence of a problem. These similarities will become more obvious when the process strategies for defining objectives are presented later in this chapter. First, however, let's review some general guidelines to follow when defining objectives. These will apply regardless of strategy.

GENERAL GUIDELINES FOR DEFINING OBJECTIVES

Until the application of these guidelines becomes second nature, it is a good idea to briefly review them prior to the commencement of any problem-solving or decision-making activity.

1. If there is a problem involved, make sure it is completely understood before attempting to formulate objectives. Don't try to decide where you want to go until you understand pretty well where you are.

2. Objectives should address results and intended outcomes, and should stay away from the "how to." Avoid discussing answers, solutions, and methods, until objectives are clearly defined. Peter Drucker said, in *The Practice of Management,* "The most common source of mistakes in management decisions is the emphasis on finding the right answer rather than the right question." Defining objectives before generating alternatives helps to avoid this mistake by providing a framework for direction.

3. Assume that you don't know everything, that new opportunities surround you waiting to be discovered, and that your opinions are probably obsolete. Proactively reassessing objectives and seeking new ones prevents stagnation. But to accomplish this in a meaningful manner requires proactive thinking. It requires a certain thirst for innovation and newness.

4. Question everything; don't take anything for granted. Frequently the most exciting opportunities can be uncovered by asking "naive" questions about the most mundane subjects or events.

5. Don't waste time setting objectives for things that are going to happen anyway. Be a manager—not a historian. The value of objectives is that they serve as tools to cause things to happen that would not otherwise occur. Sound objectives focus on outcomes that are not necessarily predictable. They then become the focal point—the guideons for action that allow the energy and effort of those affected to be channeled into productive directions.

6. Be specific. Focus as much as possible on measurable factors, tangible end-results, and quantifiable outcomes. Also be as specific as possible regarding times and deadlines. To say you want "to do something better as soon as possible" has little meaning. However, to say you want "to improve productivity an average of 10% per worker on all three production lines within six months" has very specific and clear meaning. With problem-solving activities this can make a big difference. Your objective should never be stated "to solve the problem." Rather the specific outcomes you want to achieve should be delineated.

7. The objectives you set should always be feasible. Challenge is the

source of much of the motivation people feel on the job. Accordingly, objectives should be set that challenge people. However, if objectives are set beyond the limits of what can realistically be accomplished, a defeatist attitude is certain to set in. The objectives will then become meaningless because they will be ignored. In fact everything the manager does will become less meaningful because of the lack of credibility that will set in. Credibility is as essential to the exercise of leadership as any other factor. To set objectives that are not feasible is to destroy credibility.

8. Be reasonably consistent. This is not to say one should be rigid and inflexible. Flexibility, adaptability, and the ability to innovate are critical management traits. However, on a different level consistency is equally important. People in other parts of the organization need some of the comfort that consistency in certain areas provides. Consistency should appear on several levels. Certainly any new objectives should show some consistency with other objectives, both hierarchically, and horizontally, as well as longitudinally through time. The objectives you set should be consistent with those of higher management as well as your subordinates. The hierarchy should be moving in a synchronized manner rather than in random fashion. They should also fit in with what your peers are trying to accomplish. And there should also be a certain amount of consistency between what was happening yesterday, what is happening today, and what you are trying to accomplish for tomorrow.

Your objectives should also be consistent with your own managerial responsibilities. You should not be attempting to carve out accomplishments in other's areas of concern, be they colleagues, supervisors, or subordinates. Along this vein, your objectives should also be consistent with existing organization policy and practices. If existing policy or procedure is outmoded or obsolete, accept your responsibility as a member of management to see that it is changed. If not, make sure you work within them.

The final area of consistency deals with resources. Objectives should always be consistent with available resources, including money, manpower, machine time, available time, facilities, and talent.

Within the context of these general guidelines, let's examine the strategies for defining objectives.

STRATEGIES FOR DEFINING OBJECTIVES

The four most commonly used process strategies for defining objectives are: (1) Seek, (2) Avoid, (3) Build, and, (4) Restore. They are defined as follows.

Seek

The Seek strategy means to search for new and different opportunities or possible achievements that would make a contribution to the organization. The emphasis is on newness and innovation. We are *not* talking about doing things better here. That is saved for the Build strategy. Rather we are placing emphasis on identifying new and different desired results. Although doing something better may meet the criteria of different, it falls short of meeting the criteria of doing something new or producing new results. In recalling our diagrams from earlier in this chapter and the last, we can illustrate the Seek strategy in one of two ways. In Figure 5-9 the Seek strategy is diagrammed with a problem present and without a problem present (that is, in the case of decision making only).

An advantage of the Seek strategy is that it forces innovation. It is a good practice to develop at least one or two Seek objectives every time a problem or decision is confronted. Forcing such development can be one of the most productive activities possible for fostering a spirit of innovation and development. After having developed one or two such objectives, a determination can then be made as to whether or not they should be followed through. Regardless of whether you are solving problems or making decisions, and regardless of the type of problem or decision under scrutiny, the Seek strategy should always be used.

Avoid

Avoid is used to identify potential pitfalls and problems, either as a result of past experience, present concerns, or future considerations, which can be avoided if proper priorities are established. Like the Seek strategy, Avoid should be used in every case of problem solving and decision making. After accomplishment objectives are identified, the question should be asked regarding potential situations or circumstances that should be avoided.

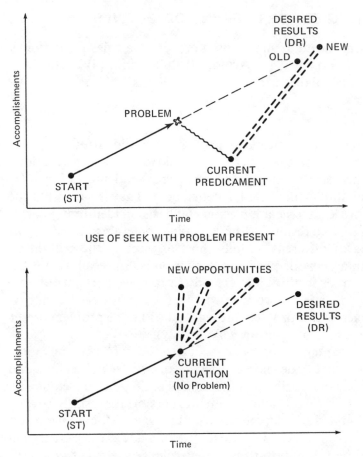

USE OF SEEK WITH PROBLEM PRESENT

USE OF SEEK IN THE ABSENCE OF A PROBLEM

FIGURE 5-9. Use of Seek Strategy in Problem Solving and Decision Making.

When solving a problem, the primary strategy selection may be Restore—its purpose to restore conditions to the desired level. The primary task then is to define what level is desired and set target dates and milestones that will help lead to this condition. However, it would be foolish to ignore the fact that new problems always bring with them new information. This new information could very well provide new insights regarding potential future problems. Good managers will take this into account and avoid becoming so bogged down with the current predicament that future problems are ignored until they reach crisis potential.

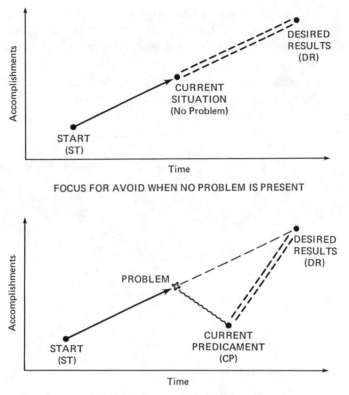

FOCUS FOR AVOID WHEN NO PROBLEM IS PRESENT

FOCUS FOR AVOID WHEN PROBLEM IS PRESENT

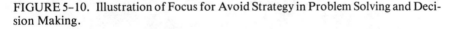

FIGURE 5-10. Illustration of Focus for Avoid Strategy in Problem Solving and Decision Making.

The focus for Avoid activities is the direction of desired results that have been already defined. It does not matter whether or not a problem exists. Look in the direction of the desired results and try to identify any outcomes that are possible but *un*desired. Set objectives that will steer clear of these undesired results, yet lead to those that are desired. Figure 5-10 shows how this can be diagrammed.

Build

To Build is to develop and capitalize on existing strengths in the organization or its operations in order that they can be exploited to the fullest extent possible.

There is and always will be a challenge for organizations to improve the way they do things. The quickest path to obsolescence and organizational demise is the course that precludes improvement. It is a fact of life that if you don't find better ways of doing things, someone else will. If that person doesn't decide to go into competition with you, eventually the idea will occur to an entrepreneur who will. That person will become your competition and put you out of business.

Perhaps the best example of ongoing building and improvement has occurred in the Bell System thoughout the United States during the twentieth century. While organizations such as the Postal Service con-

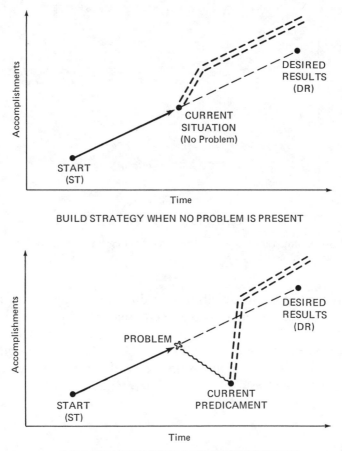

BUILD STRATEGY WHEN NO PROBLEM IS PRESENT

BUILD STRATEGY WHEN A PROBLEM IS PRESENT

FIGURE 5-11. Illustration of Build Strategy in Problem Solving and Decision Making.

tinue to provide less efficient service and struggle to "hold their own," the Bell System has lived a philosophy of proactively and deliberately searching for better ideas and ways to provide service more efficiently. This is why the cost of postage continues to rise while the cost of phone services for the average American has declined. This is also why, in spite of the fact that both are virtual monopolies, a great deal of competition has sprung up for the Postal Service and little shows as a real threat to Ma Bell.

The concept of the Build Strategy is illustrated in Figure 5-11.

Restore

Restore is the primary strategy for defining objectives in problem-solving situations. The aim is to return things to a desired level of previous mode of operation after some unexpected departure or deviation from that desired status.

Restore can be illustrated in one of two ways as shown in Figure 5-12. The first example shows activity being directed back toward the original point of departure then continuing along the previously prescribed track. The second example shows activity being directed from the place it is now to a milestone that was originally described. In this case what is being restored is not necessarily the exact same activities, but the focus of activity on the same initially defined results.

In summary, it is important to note that the first three strategies will find application most often in decision making situations where a problem has not been the stimulus to act. The fourth, the strategy of Restore, will be most frequently used for defining objectives in the presence of a problem. However, all strategies for defining objectives should be considered in all situations. This makes the strategies for defining objectives slightly different from the strategies for each of the other six steps in the Lyles Method. In the other steps one strategy is generally used to the exclusion of the others. Different strategies are better than others in different types of situations and when addressing different types of problems and decisions.

Defining objectives, however, requires a more integrated approach and thinking that is multifaceted. At all times a manager should be looking for ways to innovate, build, identify new opportunities, and be alerted to potential problems that are best avoided.

Finally, objectives focus on results, more than on method. They

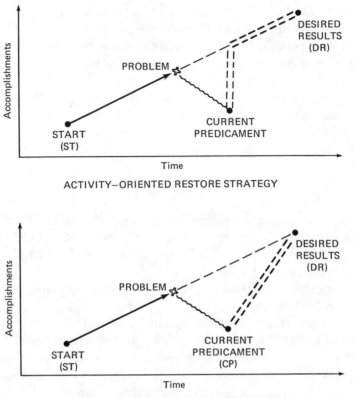

FIGURE 5-12. Illustration of Restore Strategy in Problem Solving and Decision Making.

point out the direction and detail of the outcomes that should be pursued. The actual actions to accomplish these results are developed in the next step, Generating Alternatives, which is covered in detail in Chapter 6.

6
Generating Alternatives

Generating alternatives involves much more than merely thinking up things to do. There is a difference between activities that seem like reasonably worthwhile endeavors, and alternative courses of action that are devised specifically to contribute to the accomplishment of managerial objectives. Two factors make the difference.

The first and most obvious factor contributing to the generation of meaningful alternatives is the presence of goal orientation, and the focus on results. Valuable alternatives gain their value because it is clear they will lead to the accomplishment of important end-results. Whenever the question, "Why are we doing this?" is asked, a direct and specific answer along the lines of, "Because it is contributing to the accomplishment of . . . ," should be immediately forthcoming. Never should the response be, "Because it seems like the thing to do."

The second factor has to do with creativity. Most problems and non-problem situations in management are unique. There is always something that is different in a particular set of circumstances that is unlike the characteristics of other similar circumstances. This is the major reason no one has yet been able to devise a recipe book of management actions to refer to in the solution of management problems. Thus, being able to create on an ongoing basis is the key to generating viable alternatives.

HOW TO BECOME HABITUALLY CREATIVE

Much of what is written regarding creativity places emphasis on generating the occasional big idea. In the area of problem solving, a great deal of what is written regarding creativity is oriented toward development of a single uniquely innovative idea to solve an especially perplexing problem. Accordingly, the methods presented are usually fairly cumbersome and involved. Although effective and well-grounded, it has been my experience that they do not enjoy widespread use among managers for two reasons. First, is because the participants using these methods must be trained believers. Rarely is a manager fortunate enough to have a group to work with in this type of situation all of whose members have been trained in the same method. It is not very satisfying to work through a problem using a method that must be explained and taught at the same time the problem is worked. It is also not very productive because the teaching periods detract from the productive periods, interrupting the train of thought and dampening the flow of ideas. The second reason these more elaborate methods are not used much is that major problems worth spending large amounts of time and energy solving simply don't occur very frequently. Most of the problems and decisions managers encounter are more mundane. They aren't worth the time and energy these elaborate methods require. However, this is not to say these problems won't benefit from creative input. Quite the contrary. There is tremendous potential benefit to be gained from creative input to their problems because collectively they comprise the majority of problems encountered. Thus, if a manager wants to be both practical and creative, alternative ways of fostering creative input are in order.

The best way to accomplish creative input as a matter of routine is to make creative thinking second nature to every management action. Creativity must become habitual. It must be customary rather than the exception. The manager must become so accustomed to thinking creatively that it is more comfortable to innovate than to stay in a rut. This does not mean managers must be forever cute and clever. It means they should be willing to create (i.e., to produce or bring into existence with imaginative skill) new apporaches to problems rather than relying only on their powers of recall to provide alternatives.

The following five factors, if practiced regularly, and consciously integrated into everyday activity, have proven helpful in assisting managers to be creative. They will provide the foundation from which creative actions and ideas will flow.

1. Know What Activities Stimulate Your Creative Inspiration

Just about everyone has had the experience of thinking of a particularly innovative idea or alternative when in the midst of doing something else. Usually this happens when the something else consists of routine physical activity that does not require a great deal of concentrated mental effort. Examples include walking, jogging, processing routine paperwork, gardening, driving an automobile, and making repairs around the house. A high-level government executive I know says nothing stimulates his creativity more than a trip to the museum. Fortunately his office is near the Smithsonian in Washington, DC, so he frequently strolls to the museum and has yet to come away without new ideas. Other managers I've known have learned to trigger creative moments with music, trips to the library, or meditation.

For most of us these creativity stimulating activities occur by chance. Consistently creative people, those who boast an above average level of creativity, oftentimes consciously engage in these activities when they want to stimulate creativity. When stymied by a problem, or perhaps when they are unable to think of anything other than routine courses of action, they will set the problem aside briefly and do something else, or they will continue to mull over the problem while engaging in an activity they suspect will stimulate creativity for them.

2. Regularly Stimulate Balanced Brain Hemisphere Functioning

Recent brain research has revealed a wealth of information about how the human brain operates. Researchers have discovered that the cerebrum (the largest section that rests on the top) is divided into a right and a left cerebral hemisphere. They've also discovered that the cerebrum is the part of the brain used primarily for information processing, that each hemisphere processes information differently, and each is concerned with different kinds of information. The left cerebral hemisphere is concerned mainly with words, language, logic, and reasoning. It tends to handle information sequentially, processing one piece of information at a time. The right cerebral hemisphere specializes in intuitive thinking and the ability to recognize conceptual relationships between things and events. It tends to process information simultaneously, combining different kinds of information at once. It is especially adept at handling visual information, music, and feelings.

Both hemispheres are necessary for the practice of management. However, Western society has tended to place greater value and emphasis on logic, rationality, and step-by-step approaches for both communicating and carrying out routine job responsibilities. Most educational programs are structured in very similar sequential formats. All this causes the left hemisphere in most of our brains to be more active than the right. We are thus conditioned to be more comfortable using the logical, rational, *uncreative* side of our brain. The more comfortable we get, the more we rely on it, causing a cycle of reinforcement pushing us away from the kind of brain activity that leads to innovation.

There are times when both sides of the brain work together naturally. This occurs when the circumstances lend a natural advantage to the right hemisphere (such as at a concert), when something happens to hamper processing by the left side, or when processing by the right side is directly stimulated. Sleep tends to restrict verbal processing while allowing the processing of visual information and feelings. This is why many people feel that the times just before falling off to sleep and just as they are awakening in the morning are the best times for creative inspiration. At these times the brain waves from the two hemispheres are synchronizing so as to cause a balance in brain activity. When this synchronization, or balance, occurs creative activity seems to be at its peak.

The challenge for managers lies in being able to achieve this balance in brain hemisphere functioning at times when it is most helpful. Techniques such as deep relaxation, self-hypnosis, and meditation are useful ways to accomplish balance. The key is regular and persistent use, whichever you choose for you. One or two fifteen- to twenty-minute periods should be habitually set aside each day for this type of activity. Figure 6–1 provides a more detailed comparison of the dominant characteristics of each hemisphere.

CHARACTERISTICS OF BRAIN HEMISPHERES

The right and left hemisphere of the human brain are each responsible for different kinds of thought processes and functions. The left side of the brain, which is dominant in most right-handed people, is the logical, analytical, sequential, and linear portion of the brain. The right hemisphere, which is the dominant side for more than half of all left-handed people, tends to be the intuitive, holistic, integrative, and imagery-oriented side of the brain. A brief comparison of some of the more detailed characteristics that generally describe the two hemispheres is shown below.

LEFT HEMISPHERE	RIGHT HEMISPHERE
Rational	Nonrational
Verbal, semantic	Nonverbal
Explicit	Tacit
Convergent thinking	Divergent thinking
Linear time	Lacking a sense of timeliness
Mathematical, scientific	Artistic, musical, symbolic
Objective	Subjective
Intellectual, formal	Sensuous, experiential
Literal interpretation	Metaphorical, analogical
Controlled and consistent	Emotive, affect laden
Judgmental	Willing to suspend judgment

FIGURE 6–1. Brain Hemisphere Characteristics.

3. Continuously Seek New Discovery

As children we were continually amazed and excited with the discovery of something new. We never ceased to wonder at the exciting nature of the things around us. To be truly creative requires that we once again find ways to experience that magical feeling of excitement that accompanies the joy of learning. And the learning must extend beyond the narrow boundaries of management. If you intend to be a good manager, then of course it is important to learn about management, business, and the technologies associated with the enterprise of your organization. But it is important that learning also be pursued in areas that are not so directly related to the manager's work.

Subscribe to and read journals and magazines oriented toward business and management, and also those that are oriented toward other areas. If journals in other fields intimidate you because they go into too much depth or use too much jargon, then read magazines written more for the layman such as *Psychology Today* or *Popular Science*. Articles in magazines like these are usually stimulating and thought provoking while being useful and easy to read. Some educational television programs and topically oriented specials can serve this same purpose. However, it does not make sense to rely on television alone. Monthly trips to the library just to browse and explore are also useful.

4. Structure Your Environment to Stimulate Creative Thinking

Everything around you affects your creativity. Conscious effort should be made to arrange your office in such a way as to help stimulate creativity. Abstract paintings, sculptures, and three-dimensional puzzles are the most commonly used creativity aids found in managers' offices. I've also worked with managers who find it helpful to keep pads of certain kind of paper (such as engineering graph paper), special types of pencils, drawing tools (rulers, compass, and protractor), or a microcomputer in their office. They claim some of their best ideas come when they are tinkering around with these things while working the problem.

A Bulgarian named Georgi Lozanov has discovered that certain kinds of music, in particular the Largo movements from many Baroque classical pieces, greatly enhance brain functioning. When combined with relaxation techniques, listening to this type of music can be a powerful mental stimulus. Lozanov's research has been aimed primarily at enhancing memory, or creating hypermnesia. However, in the process he discovered that these techniques also strengthen the potential of the rest of the brain as well, particularly in the area of creativity. Thus, a portable cassette recorder with an earphone and some music cassettes would be a valuable addition to your environment. An excellent music tape with seventeen minutes of Largo Baroque Music followed by a three-minute allegro is available for $12.00 from Superlearning, Inc., 17 Park Avenue, Suite 4D, New York, NY, 10016. If you'd prefer to make your own, most libraries stock record albums you can borrow. Largo movements from pieces by composers such as Bach, Corelli, Handel, Telemann, and Vivaldi are all acceptable.

5. Practice Self-Critique, Constantly Try to Improve Everything

Creative people are tinkerers. They are compulsively dissatisfied with the status quo and continuously engaged in trying to fix things. They tend to be alert to all the irritations, frustrations, and inconveniences others take for granted, and they try to fix them. After completing a task creative people will turn to those around them and ask how they did. Their purpose in asking is not to gain strokes or feed their ego, but to find out what they can do to improve. If afforded a spare moment at any time the creative person is most likely to immediately start scanning for new improvements to create. The bottom line is visible when every time a visitor comes into contact with the creative person and asks what is new, there is always something and it is always better.

6. Challenge Your Creativity as Often as Possible With Puzzles, Games, and Exercises

A large part of being creative is being able to be flexible in the kind of thought processes you apply to different problems. Some problems are resolved most effectively when convergent thinking is used. Others benefit more from divergent thinking. Then there are the kinds of problems that require not so much divergent or convergent thinking as the ability to interpret abstract relationships of one type or another. Still others require logical sequencing or patterning of data to be able to arrive at a meaningful resolution.

The same can be said of mind-challenging games and puzzles. Practicing solving these puzzles will help to keep your thinking skills sharp and ready. The more you practice, the more you use them, and the more competent you'll become.

FACTORS THAT HINDER CREATIVITY

There are a number of factors which can affect the creative processes negatively. These are actions or behavior patterns that weaken a person's ability to be creative or innovative. Understanding what these factors are and how they operate will provide insights to aid in preventing their affect and should help to stimulate healthy, ongoing, creative mind functioning. Several of these factors include:

1. *Getting Bogged Down in Tradition.* We've all been frustrated at one time or another when someone else explains that the reason for doing something is because, "That's the way we've always done it." Statements like this certainly speak to one aspect of this affliction. But the far more dangerous aspect is when the traditions are so taken for granted that no one even thinks of challenging the assumptions that support them. It is this unconscious acceptance of the given that most hampers creativity. A good way to counteract this tendency is to consciously ask on a regular basis, "Is this still the best way to do this," or, "How can things be done differently?" In other words, develop the habit of seeking alternatives as a natural matter of course.

2. *Overcertainty.* Results when a person's reactions are dictated by what they "know to be correct," rather than what is most functional to the particular situation at hand. Frequently, this is the result of stereotyping. Often people will pursue a course of action out of sheer bull-headedness, to prove they are right, rather than change their own assumptions about the way things really are. The best way to counteract this tendency is to instill the attitude that every situation is different, and times change. Because of this, there is *no* "one best way" to do things that applies in all situations.

3. *Reluctance to Play.* Some adults, and particularly business and professional people frequently get locked into very rigid, rational, unemotional—clearly adult—behavior and thought patterns. Transactional analysis theorists describe this as being "locked into an adult ego-state." The opposite to this has been shown by a great many truly creative scientists, writers, artists, and managers who often describe their work activities as games and challenges. They enjoy actively experimenting with their roles, styles, and ways of thinking and doing. In essence they play around with things, living and learning to the fullest.

4. *Low Tolerance for Ambiguity.* In order to be creative at times it is often necessary to pursue a line of thinking or course of action that is relatively unclear. In other words, there may be a sense of movement, without a crystal clear sense of either direction or outcome. When the transistor was discovered, the scientists involved with the research had no idea their specific findings related to the transistor would result from their investigations. Yet they moved ahead, trusting the process,

convinced that their competent approach would inevitably produce valid results. Of course the results were far greater than any had anticipated.

5. *Either/Or Thinking.* This type of thinking results when people limit the range of options to a finite number of altenatives, dedicated to the belief that the ultimate solution or course of action can be only one of those options, totally excluding all others. The worst case occurs when the number of options is limited to two, and they are diametrically opposed, ignoring the entire range of options on the continuum in between. Although arguments and adversary relationships can be useful in causing new data and perspectives to surface, they can be detrimental if the result is deeper entrenchment around a limited range of alternatives or positions.

6. *Reluctance to Indulge in Fantasies.* Fantasies are the product of a fertile imagination. Yet many who desire to be creative harbor a fear of fantasy that hinders the attainment of this goal. To develop a healthy ability in this regard requires using images, associations, daydreams, analogies, metaphors, and all sorts of fictional "what if's" as tools to stir up innovative thoughts. One creative achiever said it this way, "You've got to have a dream in order to have a dream come true."

7. *Fear of Taking Risks.* Although fear of failure is a part of this, it is also important to note that oftentimes creativity is stifled by the simple fear of trying something new and different simply because it is new and different and the final outcome is speculative at best. If given a choice between doing something that we're used to (and also has reasonably predictable outcomes), and doing something new and different, most of us will at least have a tendency to pursue the familiar because it is less of a risk.

8. *Lack of Emotional Involvement.* In this "rational" world in which we live, many people believe that, (1) emotions must be totally controlled if people are to work together as a group; (2) displaying emotions is a sign of immaturity; (3) show of emotions blocks clear and effective thinking; (4) emotional expressions devalue the person to whom they are directed; and/or (5) people who show emotions have little concern for the feelings of others. However, most truly great crea-

tive accomplishments have come from people who are not afraid to get emotionally involved. Emotional involvement naturally generates energy and intellectual excitement that can be very productive in tapping into full human potential.

9. *Dull Perceptions.*   In order to produce clear, vivid, innovative thoughts and ideas, it is first essential to be able to process information entering your brain in a clear and sharp manner. There's a saying among computer operators that if the information the computer puts out is bad, it's probably because the information that was put in to begin with was bad. They sum it up with the saying, "Garbage in = Garbage out." The same is true of the human mind. In order to process information about what is going on around us with some degree of accurracy (and then be able to produce some meaningful and creative output), that information must be sensed with a reasonably high degree of sensitivity and accuracy.

STRATEGIES FOR GENERATING ALTERNATIVES

The four primary strategies for generating alternatives are: (1) Brainstorm, (2) Copy, (3) Adapt, and (4) Combine. Although Brainstorm is probably the most frequently used of the four, every effort should be made to experiment with the others as often as possible to avoid becoming stale in either content or approach. Merely using different strategies in a creative process such as this one will often stimulate much richer results because it will force the thought processes out of comfortable ruts and repetitive routines.

Brainstorming

Alex Osborn developed the first formally presented ideas regarding brainstorming during the 1930s. In the half-century that has followed, the technique has gained wide acceptance and use and his original suggestions and guidelines have remained virtually unchanged. Although brainstorming as Osborn conceived it, and as it is most widely used, is a group process, the same techniques can be used by individuals acting alone with good success. The key to success, whether acting alone or brainstorming with a group, is discipline—rigorously following the ground rules. If the ground rules are not followed and the process breaks down, the results will suffer correspondingly.

Brainstorming is used to generate creative new alternative courses of action to act as raw material or "input" to the development of an action plan. It works best with groups of less than ten. The process itself is very simple. The group meets and first spends a reasonable amount of time making sure every group member fully understands the objectives of the decision and has a common vision regarding the desired end results. If they are responding to a problem, it is important everyone understand the problem, both cause and effect. Once this understanding is achieved, the members then began thinking up alternative ways to accomplish the objectives. As the alternatives are generated, one or two members of the group should write them down (on a chalkboard or flip-chart paper for all to see) as quickly as possible *as stated* by the originator. This part of the process should be intense and uninhibited, with everyone trying to develop as many new and different ideas as possible. Discussion or evaluation of individual ideas should be avoided because it will tend to slow down the process and dampen enthusiasm and creativity. The following ground rules are suggested for brainstorming sessions. They will be most effective when written out on flip-chart paper or posterboard and posted in the meeting room. They should be reviewed at the start of the session and referred to whenever any of them is being violated during the session.

1. Everyone tries their best to develop as many new and different alternatives as possible.
2. Anything goes. There is no such thing as a "bad" idea. A far-out and impractical suggestion may spur another creative and practical idea by someone else.
3. Don't evaluate, criticize, or discuss any ideas during the brainstorming process.
4. Generate as many alternatives as possible.
5. Use the ideas of others to stimulate your own thinking. Try to improve on them or combine them to come up with better approaches.
6. Encourage each other. Work as a group to develop a group product rather than getting into competition with each other.

There are a number of techniques that can be used during the brainstorming process to stimulate creative thinking by causing individual channels of thought to be directed into different avenues. Rather than presenting these to the group all at once, it will probably be more productive for the group leader to mention a couple at a time when there are lulls in the idea generating activities. These techniques for thinking along different dimensions can be triggered by using the following questions.

Can We Combine? Which of the ideas or altenatives can be blended together or combined? Can an assortment of different alternatives be devised so the total effect will be different from the individual parts?

What Existing Things Can Be Modified To Meet This Need? Can we change shape, name, sound, odor, taste, movement, sequence, or color?

Can We Magnify Anything to Create Different Alternatives? Can something be added? What about enlargements, additional ingredients, or greater frequency?

What Can Be Reduced? Is it possible to subtract or eliminate something to develop additional options? Can something be made smaller or lighter? What about slower or less frequent? Can something be split up or divided into smaller units, steps, or parts?

Are Any Opposites Feasible? What happens when we reverse direction on something? How about working backward? Can we turn something inside out or upside down?

Can We Think Of Any Substitutes? What if someone else did it? Who else might be used? What other equipment is practical? How about different times or places?

The purpose of asking any of these questions is to trigger creative and innovative thinking with a minimum of discussion and wasted time.

Most people prefer to let their brainstorming sessions run relatively free, following the ground rules, but using as little structure as possible. Results will be best of course with a relatively mature group who are used to working together. A mature group is most likely to encourage full participation and stick to the ground rules. If the group has difficulty in working this way, for example one or two members dominating the discussions, then a different more structural approach called "sequential solicitation."

Sequential Solicitation. This is designed to provide each member of the group with an opportunity to contribute, while also tending to force presentation of ideas that members might otherwise be a bit reluctant to propose. The recorders merely solicit ideas (one or more) from each member in sequence by going around the room, one at a time, giving each member an opportunity to speak in order. If a member has nothing to suggest on a given turn, he or she just says "pass" and works on developing an idea for the next turn. Although this procedure makes the process less spontaneous, it also makes it difficult for a small number of group members to dominate the discussion. It forces discussion to focus more directly on the problem and promotes greater involvement. It also discourages members from developing one "good" idea and dropping out, with the thought in the back of their mind that the problem "has been solved."

After the group runs dry—that is, no more new ideas are forthcoming—there are still several things that can be done to further stimulate thinking. One method, often referred to as the second effort technique, works as follows. When everyone has run out of ideas, have the entire group sit or mill about the room in absolute silence for three full minutes, reviewing and studying all the alternatives that have been suggested so far. Allow no talking! At the end of this time require everyone to take one more minute to develop one more idea. Then go around the room soliciting this one additional idea from each person. Quite often the very best ideas are generated during this reflective period because people have been bombarded with all the other ideas which act as a stimulus to inspire higher quality thinking when members are forced to "change gears" in their thought processes.

The Group-Individual-Group (G.I.G.). This technique is another effective way to enhance brainstorming results. It is employed by conducting a brainstorming session with the group, then breaking up for a period of time before reconvening again for renewed brainstorming activities as a group. The time between group meetings could be as short as a few hours or as long as a few days. An advantage of this approach is that it provides an incubation period for new ideas to develop. Another advantage is that it gives group members an opportunity to let their subconscious minds work the problem, increasing the probability that top-quality alternatives will be developed in greater quantity. And finally, it provides the opportunity for a fresh start at another time.

The most common problem in brainstorming is that brainstormers frequently get bogged down or entrapped by their previous experiences. This causes the brainstorming session to be more of a memory-testing exercise than an exercise in creativity. Recalling old techniques is not necessarily bad, but if it is the only source of ideas the results are bound to be bland and boring. Brainstorming is most effective when it fosters creativity and the development of *new and different* courses of action.

Copy

The word copy for most of us has a negative connotation that, unfortunately, causes us to overlook many simple and expedient alternatives that would suit many of our needs exceptionally well. Because a copied alternative does not require the time and costs of development and testing, it is usually more efficient as well.

In order to take full advantage of the copy strategy, one must first expunge any notion that copying is wrong. This is *not* to say that copyrights, patents, and such should not be respected and honored. They should be. It is to say, however, that many viable and worthwhile courses of action exist in tested and reliable form and it would be foolish and irresponsible to ignore them for the cause of originality.

"Not Invented Here Syndrome," commonly referred to as "NIH Syndrome," is one of the most costly afflictions of management. For whatever absurd reasons, many managers operate on the assumption that if they or someone who works for them did not originate an idea, then the idea has no merit. This notion usually stems from the attitude that only they or their people understand their unique predicament well enough to be able to develop a "better idea." The catch is that, even though every situation is different, none is so different as to obviate the infusion of outside ideas.

Businesses in competition with each other do a fair amount of copying merely to be able to stay in competition. Perhaps the most visible and widespread examples of this throughout the United States take place in the fast-food industry. Major hamburger chains are forever copying menu changes, service features such as drive-through windows, and promotional gimmicks to increase business. But just about anywhere goods or services are being sold direct to the public you are likely to find an abundance of successful copying taking place.

Copying will probably be most viable when dealing with operational problems. This is the area where you will most likely encounter challenges or circumstances very similar to those already encountered by someone else. Rather than spend inordinate amounts of time trying to "reinvent the wheel," so to speak, it is usually more practical to find out what "wheel" may have been invented by others and to capitalize on it as quickly as possible, building on their ideas instead of starting from scratch.

There are a number of sources of information to find out what others are doing. Trade journals, newspapers, general news magazines, television, and radio are one category of sources. Individual membership in professional societies and company affiliations with trade organizations provide additional idea-gathering opportunities. Continuing education programs, seminars, workshops, and training courses can also be worthwhile in this regard. However, standard college and university courses usually prove to be not very lucrative in this regard. They are typically oriented toward the basic information in a particular subject area and are not caught up with state-of-the-art developments in the field. Contrary to most people's assumptions, most innovation and new ideas come from the operating environment—not academe.

Adapt

Although adapt may have a connotation very similar to copy, the strategy of Adapt is quite different from the strategy of copy. Adapt as a strategy means to determine if other actions, concepts, or techniques from unrelated fields can be modified or changed to fit the needs of a particular situation. The concepts might come from history, something man-made, nature, or outer space for that matter. Many valuable and useful alternatives to business problems are the result of an astute observation of a similar type problem in some other field and the resultant adaptation of that principle to the world of work.

The following approach has worked most effectively for me in trying to generate alternatives using the adapt strategy.

1. Analyze the problem and objectives to identify major underlying themes or characteristics of the current dilemma.
2. Randomly select a referent setting or subject area that is

dramatically different from the one you are currently operating in. Stay away from subject areas that may overlap with hobbies or outside interests of the people involved. Try to pick unusual conceptual frameworks that you, and others who might be involved, are unused to thinking in.

3. Identify as many examples as possible of the themes or characteristics you defined in the first step operating in the referent setting you identified in the second step. Keep listing these examples until it is impossible to think of any more.

4. Select three or less items from your list and try to adapt the same principle to meet the needs of your current problem. If you are working with a group, you can assign different items to different individuals or subgroups to work out the adaptation. When this is completed you'll then have three viable alternatives to choose from. It is highly probable that all three will be much more creative and innovative than any of the alternatives the group will have thought of beforehand.

A recent experience I had with a client of mine should serve as a good illustrative example of how this process might work with an actual problem.

I was called in by my client, a medium-sized manufacturing company, to work with a group of midlevel managers in solving a plant-wide morale problem. The directive given the group was to develop some ways to improve the sagging morale that for some reason was afflicting everyone. My job with the group was to serve as a group leader, structuring the activities of the group and offering suggestions and injecting my expertise whenever I thought it might help. We met at the scheduled time and the meeting began, as most meetings of this type do, with a general discussion of our charter. It was apparent that all agreed that morale was on the downswing, and something needed to be done to improve it. Again like most groups in this type situation, we began brainstorming possible actions to take to improve things.

In a very short period of time it became obvious that brainstorming wasn't going to get the job accomplished. The same listlessness that was afflicting the plant as a whole had permeated the group. The ideas they suggested were dull and lifeless. After a short time the group began to realize the impassiveness of their efforts, and the spirit of the group began to decline even further. The situation was rapidly deteriorating. At that time I decided to shift from brainstorming to the strategy of adapt.

First the group went back to focus on the problem of morale. I had them analyze it to determine certain aspects of the problem that were causing people to feel the way they were. In a short time all agreed that a major contributing factor was the lack of meaningful information flow. It seemed that the grapevine was much more active, though much less accurate, than any of the formal communications procedures used by management. A lot was happening at the plant. But there were many times more rumors than there was factual data to report. Quite frequently the rumors surrounding an event so distorted reality that when the actual account was disseminated people were demoralized or gave it little credence. People felt as though management held them in low esteem and didn't care enough about them to provide timely and accurate information. All agreed that sloppy formal communications was a key contributing factor to the low morale. Having successfully accomplished the first step in the adapt strategy, we moved to step two.

Step two involves selecting a different referent setting to gather ideas relating to the theme. Examples of referent settings typically used include, nature, outer space, sports, prehistoric times, the wild West, jungles, oceans, and circus world. I have found that sports does not work very well with groups of managers in which males predominate because it is a subject they are far too familiar with, talking and/or reading about sports activities almost daily. The best effect is achieved when the subject area is less familiar. In this instance I chose the wild West.

The third step was for the group to think of as many examples as they could of communications from the wild West. Their interest piqued, they began generating ideas. The list included such items as smoke signals, pony express, telegraph, railroad, word-of-mouth, reflecting mirrors, newspapers, tent chautauquas, town meetings, county fairs, powwows, and medicine shows. With energy running high we moved into the fourth step.

During the listing process I had noticed that the idea of a pony express system had sported a positive reaction and triggered several comments from different members of the group. In an effort to take advantage of as much natural positive energy as possible, I selected this idea for the group to work with during step four. The task then was to adapt the concept of a pony express system to meet the needs of the plant.

After a few tentative moments, things started to click. They decided that there should be a network of "way stations" that could provide coverage for the entire plant, top to bottom. They set up requirements for maintaining a pool of "fresh riders" at each station so the work could be passed along without losing energy or being side tracked. Special precautions were laid out to "protect the riders" from "ambush" so the network could maintain its integrity. Recognizing that all messages could not be sent pony express, priorities were established. Some information would travel by "stagecoach" and still other information would be sent by "wagon train." Criteria were also established for transmitting certain information via "telegraph," which, translated, meant the plant public address system. Just about every predominant feature of the old pony express system had direct application to the modern-day problem when adapted.

It can be reasonably argued that an alert group could probably develop something similar without the fanfare of taking a trip to the wild West. However, it is highly unlikely they would have done such a thorough job with as much enjoyment in such a short period of time. And the results when implemented were much better because of the curiosity and interest that were aroused throughout the plant when the company's new pony express system was implemented, "riders" were selected, and so on.

The major advantage of the Adapt strategy is that it forces the abandonment of underlying assumptions regarding the current operating environment. Frequently it is these underlying assumptions about "the way things are" in the everyday environment that stifle creativity and innovation. By forcing thinking in another environment, the problem is addressed without the constraints imposed in the normal setting. This enables the possibility of developing many more solutions that are feasible, but operate on a different and acceptable set of assumptions.

One final example of Adapt in use as a strategy is based on an example told by Joe Cossman. It has to do with taking a product that was designed for one purpose and recognizing its utility in a completely different setting. A number of years ago his company introduced the sprinkling garden hose into the market. The hose was nothing more than a long, flat, plastic hose with holes punched in it at regular intervals along its entire length. Sales were going well, but took a sudden jump with an increase in orders from a large number of chicken farmers. Curious to know what possible use chicken farmers could have for a garden hose, he tracked one down and asked him. The farmer explained that a major problem chicken farmers faced was keeping their coops cool during the hot summer months. A farmer in the Midwest came up with the easy and inexpensive idea of running one of the sprinkling garden hoses the length of the coop, along the center of the roofline. When the weather turned warm, all he had to do to cool his coop was turn the water on for awhile. He submitted his idea to the chicken farmers trade magazine and everyone copied it.

Combine

Quite often, groups of things take on radically different qualities in combination, than any of the items contain individually. The same can be said of groups of people and groups of ideas. However, when we review ideas, products, processes, and the like, we frequently tend to view them sequentially, as something distinct and different from each other. Combine, as a strategy, means to integrate a number of different existing alternatives, planned actions, ideas, products, or processes to develop a synthesis more powerful than any taken alone would be.

The process for combining is perhaps the simplest of all the strategies. One merely identifies existing elements and begins to tinker with them, surmising what would result from different combinations. This is very similar to, but perhaps much less dangerous than the process used by many amateur chemists who might spend an afternoon mixing various ingredients from the chemistry set to see what reactions can be created. Quite frequently the payoff is much better however, with the rewards being reaped in terms of greater levels of efficiency, reduced duplication, and improved results.

In summary, one of the most important rules to remember when generating alternatives is one that we also use specifically for brainstorming. The rule is that evaluation and criticism should be avoided until after all alternatives have been developed. Only then should the actual deciding take place. From the list of alternatives, the best should be chosen and a plan of action developed. Chapter 7 details the specifics of how to accomplish this.

7

Developing Action Plans

Step IV in the Lyles Method, Developing Action Plans, is the stage in the process where all the important deciding transpires. It is here that various courses of action are compared and analyzed, leading to the selection of one in particular that will be implemented. At the risk of sounding trite, it is important to emphasize that this should never be the first step in either decision making or problem solving. In decision making it is important that objectives be reviewed and fresh new alternatives be identified first. Problems bring the additional demand of problem definition before either of these. One of the most impractical decisions a manager can make is to decide first and think about objectives and alternatives later. Although this kind of "Monday morning quarterbacking" may be ego satisfying for sports watchers, it has no place in the realm of practical management decision making and problem solving.

The act of choosing a course of action—actually deciding what to do—lies at the very heart of management. Being able to judge *and to choose* is what makes people managers. The surest test of personal responsibility and authority is to ask what decisions an individual can make alone without the approval, authorization, or consent of higher authority on a case by case basis. The answer to the question, "what decisions are you allowed to make?" is the most accurate description of a person's management responsibility and authority. Like no other dimension of management activity, performance as a decision maker directly and predictably affects results.

A recent article in *Fortune* magazine described the personality and style of the ten toughest chief executive officers in American business. Both interesting and provocative, the article made a vivid point regarding style and personality. Some of the most successful managers and executives are rude, abrasive, and indifferent. Although many others are compassionate, polite, and sensitive, these traits are certainly *not* common denominators for success. The same can be said of almost all dimensions used in analyzing managerial performance. Even such pioneering management theories as those developed by people such as Douglas McGregor, Blake and Mouton, and Hersey and Blanchard, although extremely helpful, fail to provide anything close to a simple answer for success. Too many other factors and contingencies intervene that prevent any "success formulas" based on specific styles of management to be devised.

Many factors such as planning, organization, and staffing have profound effects on long-range results. But once again, we are surrounded by evidence that says managers and organizations can survive without high-quality efforts in these areas. However, this cannot be said of decision making. Neither managers, nor the organizations they serve can survive without good decisions. This is not to say that bad decisions from time to time will automatically kill an organization, although many dead organizations got that way as a result of bad decisions. But it is a fact of management life that regardless of style and many other factors, managers who make good decisions tend to rise to the top and those who make bad decisions get washed out.

This is one reason why so many management experts have tried to devise sure-fire ways of making accurate decisions. Numerous attempts have been made to take the "guesswork" out of decision making. In essence, what these efforts are aimed at is taking the human judgment out of decision making. This will never be accomplished, for the following reasons. First off, almost all management decisions of any magnitude (particularly those involving people and operational matters) deal with people and human nature, which in itself is unquantifiable and unpredictable. Just look at the public opinion polls taken prior to recent major elections in the U.S. and compare them to the actual election results. See how unpredictable human nature is. The second reason is that management decisions focus on future events and no one can predict the future. No matter how well we analyze trends and project the likely consequences if various alternatives are followed, not one can consistently predict the future with any degree of certainty. And a final reason we'll never be able to take the judgment out of decision making is that there is a judgmental process that is necessary in every phase of decision making besides just the "choosing" phase. Judgment is used in determining which data are important, what variables to consider, and which time frames are relevant, to mention several points. Because judgment is used at the enabling phases of activity, we will never be able to detach ourselves when it comes time to decide. Thus, it is important to understand a few things about judgment.

JUDGMENT IN DECISION MAKING

For managers judgment is the process of forming an opinion or evaluation by discerning or comparing data. In developing action plans managers go through a judgmental process prior to formally choosing a specific course of action. The difference strategies presented for developing action plans are all aimed at making this judgmental process a conscious and deliberate activity that will help managers choose the best alternatives in different situations. Before examining the mechanics of different strategies, however, it is important to understand some of the factors that affect the judgmental process of managers.

First comes the issue of personal predilection competing with situational analysis that will lead to an optimum course of action for the present. Quite frequently decision-making judgement is relegated to certain prepotent factors the people involved are most comfortable with. In a study conducted by Dr. Alan Rowe of the University of Southern California Graduate School of Business Administration, he identified that these prepotent factors enter the judgmental processes in very visible ways. His studies involved managers from Belgium, Denmark, England, France, Holland, Iran, Norway, and the United States. They revealed that although many factors influence decisions when personal considerations are involved, usually a single factor emerges that tends to be given an inordinate amount of influence and dominates the selection. This appears to become more pronounced the higher one goes in management. Rowe found that at higher levels of management more factors had to be taken into account when making decisions. However, the study showed that when personal or behavioral decisions were involved, managers tended to revert to a single prepotent factor based on personal preference, regardless of how detailed the analysis and regardless of the number of factors examined. It seems as though it might be easy to create the illusion that the decision making process is objective and all encompassing when, in fact, it is not. One of the valuable traits that is hardest to develop is to argue and examine alternatives with the objectivity required to find the best answer rather than the answer one is most comfortable with.

Another factor affecting judgement is the perception of risk, predictability, and uncertainty. Dr. Rowe found that although managers are aware that risks exist, they seldom make explicit estimates of the identifiable risks involved in their decisions. More typically, they usually choose between a limited number of alternatives, using lack of time as an excuse for not examining potential consequences in greater detail. My work with managers has certainly verified this. However, I think another issue plays on this. It deals with the fact that most people don't know how to deal with data in a way that allows them to be comfortable in choosing a course of action based on what the data might indicate. Because they're not comfortable with predictions, risk, and uncertainty, they gain comfort by choosing a course of action familiar to them. This usually turns out to be a course of action that either worked for them in the past or meets a personal need in the present. To avoid this rut it is important to understand some things about probability and uncertainty and to learn to recognize when it is helpful to try to assess probable consequences and when not to.

A number of years ago I was an officer aboard a ship sailing in the South China Sea when we received an S.O.S. distress signal from a sinking Taiwanese merchant ship. The ship sank before we arrived on the scene, but because we had reason to believe there might be survivors, we searched the area for several days. During our search we first found an empty life raft, then an empty lifeboat, and on the third day, a lifeboat with a single survivor. He told the following story.

"The day after we set sail we encountered a heavy storm. Although we were loaded beyond the safety limits of the ship, we continued ahead, trying to make the best time possible so our voyage would be profitable. The storm got worse with high winds and gigantic waves smashing over our ship. During the middle of the night we began taking on water when the storm ripped a number of hatch covers from the ship. Soon we were taking on water faster than the pumps could expel it. Eventually the water flooded the engine room deep enough so the pumps and engine could not work.

"The Captain called all the crew together on the bridge and explained our predicament. We were sinking, drifting helplessly out of control, and the storm was bad and getting worse. He had sent the S.O.S., but had no idea when help might arrive. He could radio no more because the power was completely gone. He gave orders to prepare to abandon ship. As he did so, a huge wave crashed along the side of the ship and tore the metal lifeboat cannister away, stanchions and all. We watched in awed silence as the raft inflated about twenty yards away and bobbed off like a cork, disappearing into the churning seas. This left us with two old wooden lifeboats and twenty-six crew aboard. Without a word we started completing the chores for abandoning ship. We gave our passports and important papers to the Captain who loaded them into his briefcase and placed it aboard the first lifeboat. When a lull in the storm came along we cranked the lifeboat out and began to lower it by hand. Just then a violent wave ripped down the side of the ship and stripped lifeboat, lines, and tackle away, tossing them into the sea. It drifted slowly away. We watched helplessly as it took with it much of our hope. Our attention was drawn to the final life raft. Carefully we began to lower it. Near the end of its descent the ship heaved out of rhythm with the water causing the boat to smack hard against the water. When the ship then raised and the water lowered, the sudden yank on the after line caused it to part leaving only the forward line to connect the lifeboat to the ship. Soon the lifeboat began to get battered against the side of the ship, trailing on its short lowering line. Rather than see the boat reduced to splinters, the Captain decided to cut it loose.

"In the few moments it lay close beside the ship, panic set in that each crew member was faced with a decision. Should they jump overboard, try to reach the lifeboat, which would surely not sink, or stay with the much larger, but slowly sinking ship, hoping she would stay afloat until help arrived? Shouting arguments ensued. Finally, I jumped. I struggled through the water and barely made it to the lifeboat. I shouted for others to try, but the distance had increased and they would not. About two hours later, from a distance of half a mile, I watched the ship sink with twenty-five souls aboard. Three days later a rescue ship spotted me and I was saved."

The story presents an interesting study in decision-making judgment. One man jumped, accepting an immediate risk and still unknown consequences while twenty-five did not. Obviously, at the time of the decision, all twenty-six thought they were making the correct judgment. Only days later, when the one was rescued, did the correctness of his decision bear itself out. Now the question to ask is whether this could have been predicted in advance. Is there any way to compute the probability of survival for any of the crew members, and thus quantify their decision in such a way as to give them a convincing course of action to pursue? Not in this case. Quantifiable probabilities are only relevant when the events being considered are going to occur fairly frequently, and in which all outcomes can be expressed quantitatively. A coin toss would be a good example. Each time you toss the coins, there are only two possibilities, heads or tails, and there is an equal chance that either will come up. The case of the sailor and the lifeboat, however, is different. The variables are *not* quantifiable, many are unknown (such as how near help might be), and the event is unique in the lives of those involved. Even if all aboard would have survived, this or a similar event is not likely to recur. Thus, this decision, like most management decisions, involves uncertainty.

Where uncertainty is involved, probability statistics and quantifications are of little help. Current research is showing that even in areas where statistics are available to help predict outcomes of decisions and events, people tend to ignore them. People tend to react to such decisions in ways best known to themselves. As discussed in Chapter 2, these ways frequently involve heuristics that channel judgement down the wrong path or bring the wrong criteria into play. For this reason, the strategies presented later in this chapter for developing action plans focus on methods for bringing the issues into focus to facilitate competent judgment. By design, they are not strategies aimed at quantifying the data or the decisions or for projecting probabilities of success or failure for different action plans. Their aim is to improve the quality of the judgmental processes used in decision making.

Before studying the strategies, however, here is a worthwhile set of ground rules to remember when using them.

Ten Commandments for Choosing A Course of Action

Regardless of strategy or type of problem or decision under scrutiny, these ten axioms should be followed.

1. *Focus On The Total End Result To Be Achieved.* A friend who is a manufacturing manager once expressed his frustration with his company's decision-making practices as follows. "The problem around here," he said, "is that people decide to start doing things before they ever get a clear picture of where we're going. The result is we're constantly changing direction and making modifications to the extent that our company's manufacturing philosophy could best be described as 'pound to fit and paint to match.' If only once we could know for sure where we were headed before we started, we'd be a heck of a lot more productive."

2. *Never Accept Your Final Choice As Being Final.* New information, events, and circumstances drive new decisions. Many managers feel that reversing or changing a decision after it has been announced, may be interpreted as a demonstration of poor planning or indecisiveness. They then find it impossible to admit it when it's time to change their minds. Quite frequently a course of action that was sound when decided upon becomes unsound because of changing circumstances. The consequences of steadfastly following an unsound course of action could be worse than the repercussions one might encounter in changing it.

3. *At Least 80% of the Time Choose an Alternative Other Than the First One Thought Of—You Can Almost Always Do Better!* Countless experiments have revealed that first solutions are almost never the best. For this reason it is best to defer acceptance of the first solution until as many alternatives have been thought of as possible, and each has been examined from a positive as well as critical viewpoint.

4. *Don't Do Anything Solely Because It Worked Once Before. Choose Actions that are Clearly Justified Based on the Demands of the Current Situation.* Problems that appear to be similar on the surface most often prove to be radically different when analyzed in depth. In any but the most static organizations, priorities and direction change

---

TEN COMMANDMENTS FOR CHOOSING A COURSE OF ACTION

1. Focus on the total end-result to be achieved.
2. Never accept your final choice as being final.
3. At least 80% of the time, choose an alternative other than the first one thought of—you can almost always do better.
4. Don't do anything solely because it worked once before. Choose actions that are clearly justified based on the demands of the current situation.
5. Never follow the advice of experts unless the advice completely makes sense to you.
6. Always take heed of your own intuition. A hunch is a conclusion based on facts you previously observed and stored.
7. Remember that once you act, things will change. Always be prepared to deal with new circumstances and to respond to new information.
8. Be bold rather than timid. Major changes are easier to implement and much more likely to take hold than minor changes.
9. Assess the needs and priorities of those around you and design your action plan to be supportive of them.
10. Take plenty of time to decide. Haste does tend to make waste (particularly in management decisions), so don't rush things.

R. I. LYLES

---

with time, making the demands of similar problems quite different. Competent managers will make sure "real time" criteria for evaluating courses of action are established and used.

5. *Never Follow the Advice of Experts Unless the Advice Completely Makes Sense to You.* Experts in a particular field have typically become expert because they have studied a specialty. As such they tend

to take a limited view of problems. Because today's problems are complex and specialized, a manager must frequently solicit expert advice in certain areas to be able to understand problems and decisions. However, this advice should not automatically decide the course of action. The manager should ultimately decide the course of action based on what makes sense personally, after having tempered the expert advice with the manager's own experience, the current knowledge of the organization's needs and priorities. The manager is the person most likely to see the big picture.

6. *Always Take Heed of Your Own Intuition. A Hunch is a Conclusion Based on Facts You Previously Observed and Stored.* If it is likely that you've accumulated facts and information about this type of situation in the past, and if you have found out all you can about the current situation, and as a result have a strong hunch, you should probably go with it. Hunches and a strong intuition are different from hopes and wishful thinking. A hunch about a lottery or slot machine should not be trusted because there is no way you could have accumulated facts or data about the odds.

7. *Remember That Once You Act, Things Will Change. Always Be Prepared To Deal With New Circumstances and Information.* It is virtually impossible in large, complex organizations to act without triggering some kind of reaction that will alter the situation in some meaningful way. For this reason, troubleshooting is included as a formal activity in the Lyles Method. However, it is also important to take this dynamic into account when developing action plans as well. Everything you do will affect the organization somehow. Often, the result will be totally unexpected and undesirable. Equally as often, however, the results will be positive and carry unforeseen opportunities. The decision maker should be prepared to deal with both by developing action plans with built-in flexibility. Avoid letting them be so rigid they become fragile.

8. *Be Bold Rather Than Timid. Major Changes Are Easier to Implement and More Likely to Take Hold Than Minor Changes.* Norms are to organizations like habits are to individuals. Once these comfortable patterns of behavior are established, it is difficult to nudge people away from them. But if you disrupt the entire life-style, then carefully manage the settling-in process you are much more likely to bring about lasting change.

Recently the newly hired training director for a county government contacted me to conduct management training for midlevel managers in the county organization. One of her top priorities was that the training be scheduled for just a few hours a day once a week so the training wouldn't "interfere" with their work. I countered that one of the goals of the training was to change their behavior and it might be helpful to have a disruption to help these changes occur. Because she wanted the training to be more timed—she wasn't really looking for it to change things—I declined to conduct the program.

9. *Assess the Needs and Priorities of Those Around You and Design Your Action Plan to be Supportive of Them.* At a recent banquet for the managers of a fairly good-sized manufacturing company, I found myself seated near the president of the company. He was relatively young for the position and had a widespread reputation for having worked his way to the top so quickly. During the course of the evening the inevitable question was presented to him. He was asked to what he attributed his fast and successful climb up the career ladder. After reflecting for a moment he said that he felt if it was any one thing, it was because he always looked at those above him, below him, and beside him to see what they were trying to do, and did everything he could to get them all promoted. "Then," he said, "with everyone around me getting promoted, I just sort of went with the flow!" See Chapter 2, p. 25, for advice on how to be a better camel builder.

10. *Take Plenty of Time to Decide. Haste Does Tend to Make Waste (Particularly in Management Decisions), So Don't Rush Things.* Of course, many decisions can be made immediately. For such decisions, procrastination leads to inefficiency. Making many decisions late is the same as not making them at all. Opportunities can be lost and more problems created. On the other hand, important decisions should not be rushed. Some situations improve with time. And frequently our understanding of some situations and alternatives improve with time.

Although these factors will not guarantee success in every case, if you use them, being sensitive to the issues they raise, you will most certainly improve the overall quality of the action plans you develop. Here are several strategies to use in developing action plans.

STRATEGIES FOR DEVELOPING ACTION PLANS

The Primary Strategies for Developing Action Plans are: (1) Compare, (2) Force field analysis, (3) Prioritize, (4) Subjective Evaluation. Each one will be explained separately along with guidance about when and how to use it.

Compare

To review and examine the quality of various alternatives to find the best one, either when compared to each other or when compared to some set of criteria related to objectives of a decision, then to develop an action plan based upon the alternative(s) deemed to be the best. Most decision tables and forced-choice matrix approaches fall into this category.

The simplest means of comparison is to compare each alternative to each of the others. This would be helpful in the kind of situation where there were a large number of alternatives which all met the established criteria and the decision maker was having difficulty selecting the best of the group. A lined box would be drawn with as many lines along one side and the top as there were alternatives. Then all the alternatives would be listed along the side and top of the box as shown in Figure 7-1.

	Altern. #1	Altern. #2	Altern. #3	Altern. #4	Altern. #5	Altern. #6	Altern. #7	TOTAL
Alternative #1		1	3	1	1	6	1	4
Alternative #2			2	4	2	6	2	3
Alternative #3				3	5	6	3	3
Alternative #4					4	6	4	3
Alternative #5						5	7	2
Alternative #6							6	5
Alternative #7								1

FIGURE 7-1. Comparing Alternatives to Each Other.

Taking each alternative down the side, one at a time, compare it to each of the other alternatives listed across the top to determine which of the two is best. For example, you would compare #1 to #2, #1 to #3, #1 to #4, and so on across the box. After making each comparison, enter the number of the best alternative in the box where the corresponding lines intersect. In the example shown, #1 was better than #2 so in that box a #1 was entered. Then #3 appeared better than #1 so #3 was entered. Then #1 was better than #4 so #1 was entered. These individual comparisons were continued until the entire upper right-hand portion of the table was filled. Only the upper right-hand portion is completed, since it would be redundant to repeat the comparisons in the lower left hand portion and it is meaningless to compare the alternatives to themselves. After completing the comparisons, add the number of times each alternative's number appears in the box to determine the ranking of the alternatives. The alternatives with the highest numbers should receive the most consideration and those with the zeros should be discarded.

Upon completion of this process it should now be fairly obvious to those who participated which are the stronger and which are the weaker alternatives. Be careful to avoid using the final numerical rankings as absolute rankings. This method, because of all the separate judgments required, simply is not that precise. However, it will very quickly put the issues in their proper perspective and focus attention on the strongest alternatives which can now be refined into a specific course of action.

A second method of comparing consists of comparing alternatives to criteria. It is used when there are both a large number of alternatives and a large number of different types of criteria to be satisfied. A decision table similar to the previous one is drawn. A difference here is that the alternatives are listed down the side and the criteria are listed across the top. In its simplest form, each alternative is compared to each of the criteria to determine whether or not the alternative meets the criteria, as shown in Figure 7-2.

A "Y" for yes is placed on the line below the criteria if the alternative in question meets the criteria. An "N" for no is entered if the alternative does not meet the criteria. A ranking of alternatives is then determined by counting the number of Ys each alternative received. The more Ys, the stronger the alternative.

In working with this method many managers frequently find that

	Criteria #1	Criteria #2	Criteria #3	Criteria #4	Criteria #5	Criteria #6	Criteria #7	TOTAL
Alternative #1	Y	N	Y	Y	N	N	N	3
Alternative #2	N	Y	N	N	Y	N	Y	4
Alternative #3	N	Y	Y	N	N	Y	Y	4
Alternative #4	Y	N	N	N	Y	N	N	2
Alternative #5	Y	Y	N	Y	N	Y	Y	5
Alternative #6	N	Y	Y	Y	Y	Y	Y	6
Alternative #7	N	N	N	N	N	Y	N	1

FIGURE 7-2. Comparing Alternatives to Criteria.

two variations provide both greater specificity and more realistic comparisons. One variation deals with using a scale other than the Y and N when comparing alternatives. The other involves ranking or prioritizing the criteria. Let's first examine the use of a scale other than the Y and N.

The absolute yes or no is quite frequently inaccurate because some alternatives, although they might satisfy the criteria, would not satisfy it as well as some of the others. For example, let's assume the boss wants everyone in the plant to know how much he appreciates their efforts during the past year. There are lots of ways of doing this, but let's examine just two possibilities. One is to announce his appreciation over the public address system during lunch hour. The other is to give them a bonus with a small note of appreciation and let them off a few hours early on Christmas Eve. Although both alternatives would satisfy the criteria of getting the message across, giving them both a Y does not give a valid comparison of the two. Instead of using the Yes/No responses, a five-point response will be much more meaningful. The scale would go from 0 to 4 as follows:

0	1	2	3	4
Does not satisfy criteria		Average		Meets criteria very well

If it did not satisfy the criteria, the alternative would get a 0. If it barely met it, a 1 would be entered in the box below the criteria. A 2 would be the midpoint, indicating an average level of satisfaction. A 3 would be above average, and a 4 would indicate a high level of anticipated effectiveness. Figure 7–3 illustrates what a decision table using this method would look like.

Use of the five-point response scale for comparing alternatives takes into account that different alternatives will have different effects in satisfying the criteria. However, it does not account for the fact that different criteria will frequently have different levels of importance to the decision. One obvious differentiation that occasionally surfaces is that some criteria must absolutely be met and others are simply "nice to have." In this case all the absolute criteria are listed first, separate from the "nice to haves." See Figure 7–4 for an example.

	Criteria #1	Criteria #2	Criteria #3	Criteria #4	Criteria #5	Criteria #6	Criteria #7	TOTAL
Alternative #1	2	4	1	2	4	3	2	18
Alternative #2	4	4	3	0	1	3	2	17
Alternative #3	2	1	3	4	0	2	3	15
Alternative #4	3	2	4	2	3	1	2	17
Alternative #5	1	4	3	1	2	3	2	16
Alternative #6	3	4	3	2	4	3	2	21
Alternative #7	2	1	0	1	3	2	4	13

FIGURE 7–3. Variable Scale for Meeting Criteria.

	MUST HAVE			NICE TO HAVE				
	Criteria #1	Criteria #2	Criteria #3	Criteria #4	Criteria #5	Criteria #6	Criteria #7	TOTAL
Alternative #1	2	3	2	3	1	2	3	16
Alternative #2	3	1	2	2	3	2	3	16
Alternative #3	2	0	1	1	0	2	1	discard
Alternative #4	4	3	4	2	3	3	2	21
Alternative #5	3	2	4	4	3	2	3	21
Alternative #6	1	3	1	3	2	2	1	13
Alternative #7	0	1	1	2	1	1	2	discard

FIGURE 7–4. Absolute and Conditional Criteria.

After each alternative has been compared to each criterion, an action plan is developed that satisfies all the absolutes and includes the best coverage of the "nice to haves."

Another situation arises when there are no absolutely necessary criteria, but some of the criteria are clearly more important than others. In this case you could weight the criteria according to their importance in such a way that the weightings would influence the overall rankings of the alternatives. For example, assume you have six criteria, two of which are of critical importance, two are very important, and two are important, but not nearly as much so as the others. You could then weight the two most important with a 3, the next most important with a 2, and the least important with a 1. After comparing each alternative to each criterion using the 0–4, five-point response scale previously described, you could multiply the values for each criterion by the weighting factor for the criteria. In other words you would multiply all the responses in the first two columns by 3, and the second two columns by 2, before adding them to determine an alternative's ranking value. Because the last two columns were weighted with a 1, it is not necessary to multiply them at all prior to adding. In this case if an alternative were compared to the six criteria with the following result,

#1	#2	#3	#4	#5	#6
2	1	3	2	0	4

its ranking value would be computed as follows:

$$
\begin{array}{cccccc}
3 & 3 & 2 & 2 & 1 & 1 \\
\times 2 & \times 1 & \times 3 & \times 2 & \times 0 & \times 4 \\
\hline
6 + & 3 + & 6 + & 4 + & 0 + & 4 \quad = 23
\end{array}
$$

giving a total score of 23.
See Figure 7–5 for a fully detailed example.

In summary then, the comparison strategy is used either to compare alternatives to each other when a large number meet the criteria, or to compare large numbers of alternatives to large numbers of diverse criteria to arrive at a course of action.

	X3		X2		X1			
	Criteria #1	Criteria #2	Criteria #3	Criteria #4	Criteria #5	Criteria #6	Criteria #7	TOTAL
Alternative #1	3	2	2	1	4	3	1	29
Alternative #2	2	4	3	1	4	2	3	35
Alternative #3	4	3	2	0	1	3	1	28
Alternative #4	2	0	1	2	0	2	2	16
Alternative #5	1	2	3	0	3	4	2	24
Alternative #6	3	3	2	1	0	4	3	31
Alternative #7	3	4	2	3	1	4	4	40

FIGURE 7–5. Assigning Variable Weights to Criteria.

FORCE FIELD ANALYSIS

To evaluate each alternative in terms of the factors (or forces) that would act in its favor and to its detriment. The alternative with the most factors in its favor and the least to its detriment would be chosen for the basis of the action plan. The action plan would then be developed using each of the identified factors as the primary considerations.

Benjamin Franklin was probably the first person in modern times to use and advocate this type of approach for evaluating various alternatives and developing a course of action. His method was to write a proposed course of action across the top of a sheet of paper, then divide the remaining portion in half by drawing a line down the middle from top to bottom. One side he would label "PRO" and the other "CON." Then over the course of several days he would list in pencil all the reasons he could think of for and against the proposed course of action. By allowing the process to extend over several days, he was able to mull over all the factors in depth and to examine the issues from different perspectives as he went about his other chores. As new ideas came to him, he would add them to the list. If he figured out a way to circumvent or eliminate a negative factor, he would erase it from the list. The result was a very clearly conceived course of action that had been analyzed in detail. Of course the quality most surely was much better than if he had merely looked at several alternatives and chosen one. If he had several alternatives to consider, he used the same process, laying out a separate sheet of paper for each alternative.

Many managers still use Franklin's technique today. Although there are several variations which might be helpful in different situations, one variation is especially helpful in group decision-making situations where there are a number of alternatives to consider. Each alternative is written across the top of a piece of flip-chart paper, with the remainder of the paper divided into two columns, pro and con. The sheets of paper are then taped to the wall around the meeting room. Everyone is given a felt-tipped marker and asked to write down every argument they can think of for and against each alternative. This gets all the arguments into the open and puts them all into perspective much quicker and better than a group discussion. The discussion now takes place, but it is much easier to manage, with the flip-chart sheets serving as a focal point. Advantages and disadvantages can be discussed with

FORCE FIELD ANALYSIS
WORKSHEET

ALTERNATIVE: _____

_____

_____

ADVANTAGES   DISADVANTAGES

FIGURE 7-6. Sample Force Field Analysis Worksheet.

little redundancy. Unnecessary discussion is minimized because the visual comparison of alternatives helps the group better understand the issues.

Another variation commonly used today provides greater insight into why this strategy is called Force Field Analysis. In this case the factors on each side are listed with vectors (arrows) drawn next to them pointing in either the positive or negative direction to indicate the driving power or force they are considered to have in implementing the alternative. The vectors can be drawn with varying lengths to show different magnitudes for the different factors. A factor that is considered to have a strong effect would have a long vector next to it, and those factors considered to have lesser impact would have correspondingly shorter vectors next to them (See Figure 7-7).

FORCE FIELD ANALYSIS WORKSHEET
USING VECTORS

ALTERNATIVE: Introduce new product XYZ into market nationwide
within one year.

FORCES HELPING	FORCES HINDERING
Good product	Customer resistance
Strong profit potential	Limited market
Cost competitive	Unpredictable market
Strong customer appeal	Different from past successful products
Popular with retailers	New marketing channels
Sales force likes the product	Large initial cost
Company has an established reputation	Competition likely to join in after time
Advertising can be piggy-backed with other advertising efforts to reduce costs initially	
Top management believes in the product	
New product would help company morale	

FIGURE 7-7. Sample Force Field Analysis Worksheet With Vectors.

For those desirous of even greater precision, the vectors can be assigned numerical values to connote strength. It is common to use a scale of 0 to 100, with 0 equating to an insignificant strength or effect a factor would have on the alternative in question, and 100 equating to overpowering strength. Those using this method like to then add the values of the vectors on each side to gain some sense of whether all factors taken together tend to weight heaviest for or against the alternative (See Figure 7–8).

Then each factor can be analyzed along with the course of action to see whether the course of action can be modified to account for the factor. Quite often, all the major restraining forces can be eliminated simply by modifying the course of action in ways that take them into consideration. Using the Force Field Analysis strategy this way, it becomes a dynamic and effective planning tool for developing a course

FORCE FIELD ANALYSIS WORKSHEET
USING WEIGHTED VECTORS

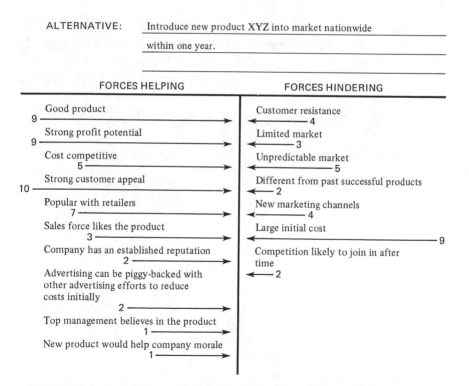

FIGURE 7–8. Sample Force Field Analysis Worksheet Using Weighted Vectors.

of action that takes into account multiple factors that might affect the intended outcome.

Prioritize

To take a large number of alternatives and prioritize them against a single criterion or a very limited set of criteria, such as time constraints, cost, or popularity. For example, there might be a situation where ten or twenty possible alternatives exist and all would be desirable. However, there may be a single constraint, such as budget limitations, that prevent the manager from implementing all the alternatives at once. Cost effectiveness would then be established as the overriding priority. Each alternative would then be rated on some type of cost-effectiveness scale. The most cost effective would take first priority, the next most cost effective would take second priority, and so on, until the entire list of alternatives was ranked. The course of action, then would be to implement the top priority item first and work down the list.

Another example would be the case where there are a large number of alternatives, but insufficient staff to implement them all at once. If all were anticipated to have equal value to the organization, they would be given priority according to the time it would take to implement them. Those taking the least time would be implemented first, gradually working down the list until everything was accomplished.

Subjective Evaluation

To work without formula or structure to weigh all possible options, taking into account intangible as well as tangible variables, to arrive at a course of action best fitting the needs of the situation. It is different from "muddling through" in that the issues are addressed directly and in a well-managed process. It is different from decision making by consensus in that all the plans are worked out in detail.

The greatest challenge in using subjective evaluation is to avoid allowing the range of options or the criteria for evaluating the options from becoming too narrow. There is a danger in using subjective evaluation that, at least in the minds of those involved, the range of considerations might narrow to very limited extremes. Semanticists refer to this phenomenon as a tendency toward *two-valued orientation*. In the previous chapter we referred to a variation of this tendency as

SAMPLE FORM FOR ESTABLISHING PRIORITIES

ALTERNATIVES	COST	TIME	PRIORITY

FIGURE 7-9. Sample Form to use in Establishing Priorities, Using Cost and Time as Criteria.

either/or thinking. When developing action plans the dangerous aspect of this tendency arises when the decision-making process degenerates into a limited number of criteria that do not adequately represent reality. The worst cases occur when the criteria are divided into only two categories such as good or bad, right or wrong, okay or not okay. Although easier to consider than a multivalued orientation, the two-valued orientations rarely serve the needs of managers.

A popular analogy regarding this tendency compares the two-valued orientation to a light switch and the multivalued orientation to a water faucet. Tell someone their lights are on and they understand pretty well what you mean. Tell them their water faucet is on and the meaning is less clear. It could mean the faucet is dripping or gushing. The world of management has operating characteristics that more closely resemble the water faucet than the light switch.

There will be management decisions that are limited to only two distinct possibilities. There will be others whose merits can only be judged against two opposing criteria. But most will not be. Because of this great care must be taken to ensure that integrative thinking is used to assure that everything that should be considered is considered and all factors are dealt with in their proper perspective.

Most of the time, the strategy of Subjective Evaluation will be used when making decisions in groups. One of the easiest ways to control group behavior and gain the type of performance desired when working with groups is to establish ground rules. The ground rules should be stated, reviewed prior to commencement of the group activity, and posted somewhere in the meeting room for all to see and for easy reference during the group activity. Different ground rules apply to different tasks and situations. The following ground rules will help group decision-making processes when using the strategy of Subjective Evaluation.

1. *Actively consider all alternatives.* There is a tendency among groups to gradually drop from discussion, and therefore from consideration, some of the alternatives under consideration without formally deciding to do so, and often without being aware that it is happening. If an alternative loses its appeal, a conscious decision should be the only act that will cause it to be deleted.

2. *Actively take into account all criteria.* The tendency toward two-valued orientation, to the extent it is present among individuals, is exaggerated in group activity. Multivalued orientation and attitude must be maintained. This means that care must be taken to avoid allowing the personal agendas of one or two group members to dominate the decision-making process.

3. *View differences of opinion as helpful.* When different opinions are presented the opportunity for learning is enhanced along with the

possibility that more people will see the big picture. Debates cause new information to be presented and almost always lead to a deeper level of understanding by everyone in the group. Differences of opinion provide energy and insights that are impossible to stimulate with complete concurrence.

4. *Avoid arguing just to win the argument.* There is a difference between arguing to get to the truth of the matter (to find out what the best answer really is), and arguing to win your point at any cost (with the foregone conclusion that no matter what anyone else says, you'll stick by your belief). Part of the difference is common sense. Another part is in being open to influence and in being a good listener. But the biggest difference is in the quality of the final results that are achieved. Those who argue to find the best answer, regardless of whether or not it agrees with their original position, will do best in the long run.

5. *Don't agree just to be agreeable.* No one in a decision-making group should ever go along with the group when they are in firm disagreement with the group solely to avoid creating dissonance, tension, or irritation. To do so is to single-handedly abrogate the responsibilities that the individual has to the group. If it was known in advance that everyone would agree with every point, there would be no value to using a group-oriented process. Not everyone will find something to disagree with in every case, nor should anyone actively try to disagree for the sake of disagreement. But when differences of opinion do arise, they should be raised and discussed.

6. *Don't take numerical shortcuts.* Using Subjective Evaluation in a group can be tedious, time consuming, and often stressful. Because of this, a tendency among group members often arises to want to take shortcuts. Methods such as voting, or assigning numerical values, and averaging are often proposed. If it honestly appears that this might be more productive, then use another strategy. If, however, subjective evaluation is the best strategy, then stick with it. Any of these other shortcuts will almost always turn out to be the long cut in the long run.

7. *Encourage everyone to participate.* The surest way to subvert the group process is to allow it to proceed without the full participation of everyone involved. This is not to say that everyone should be talking all the time. However, although it must be recognized that different people participate differently, everyone should have the opportunity to take part in the process in such a way that his/her unique contribution is taken advantage of.

Any time group decision-making techniques are employed, the

ACTION PLAN

Objectives: _____

_____

_____

_____

Specific Actions	Who	Cost	By When

FIGURE 7-10. Sample Format for Action Plan.

situation should be analyzed first to determine if it will be cost effective to use a group. If quality or acceptability will be affected enough to warrant the cost, then use a group. If a group is used just because everyone wants to take part, or because someone feels they should take part for some abstruse reason, then don't use the group.

AFTER THE CHOICE IS MADE—WHAT YOUR FINAL ACTION PLAN SHOULD BE

Certain risks are encountered when talking about form or structure for anything that happens in management. First is the risk that someone will embrace whatever form or structure is proposed, label it *the* way to do things, and launch a campaign to transform everything within that person's sphere of influence so that it will conform to the structure. The second risk is that people will see the form and structure, adapt to it, and abandon any instinct for creativity they may have harbored prior to encountering the form. Of course, when thought of directly, both of these risks seem as if they are probably more imagined than real. My experience indicates the contrary. I've encountered far too many people who behave in these ways to discount the likelihood of these risks taking place.

The form for presenting your finally developed action plan is nothing more than a suggestion. It is one example to give you some ideas about how you might best present your action plans. If offers minimal structure, yet adequate organization, so that the anticipated activities can be understood with a minimum amount of ambiguity and a sufficient amount of specificity. The specificity most important is that regarding time, cost, end results, and accountability. All else amounts to justification and can be attached if so desired, but is usually not necessary. The form is presented in Figure 7–10.

8
Troubleshooting

The most efficient problem solving possible is problem solving in advance—"solving" problems before they become problems. This means taking care of problems (or their causes) before they interfere with anything.

Troubleshooting should be introduced into a manager's practices in two places. First, it should always be the fifth formal step in problem-solving and decision-making activity as outlined in the Lyles Method. Immediately after the action plan is developed, time should be taken for a detailed critical review of the plan to identify potential problems. The second area in which troubleshooting should be applied is in the ongoing thought processes of the manager's everyday activities. A constant look forward to anticipate potential problems is a wise investment of time and mental energy.

TROUBLESHOOTING AS A STEP IN PROBLEM SOLVING AND DECISION MAKING

Troubleshooting as a step in the Lyles Method is separate and distinct from the analysis of advantages and disadvantages or the weighing of "pros and cons" used in developing an action plan. In that phase of activity the emphasis was on comparing alternatives to each other, to your objectives, or to some other criteria. Strengths and weaknesses were discussed in the context of the decision or problem under scrutiny. Now it is time to broaden our perspective and see what potential problems are likely to be encountered when our action plan is implemented that have not yet been considered. We have already evaluated the alternatives regarding one set of factors, now it is time to evaluate our action plan in light of the total situation.

It is easy for the manager to get locked into a one-dimensional mode of thinking and to thereby oversimplify his/her relationships with other aspects of the total organization. Maybe this results because of

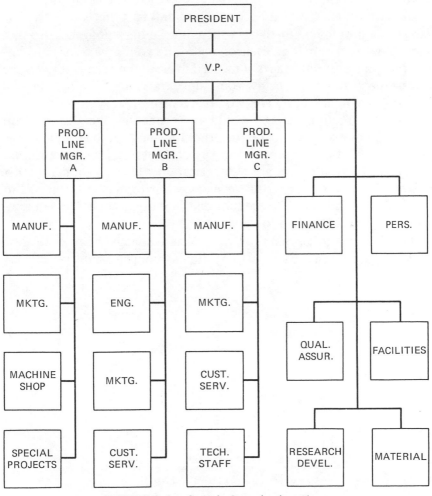

FIGURE 8-1.   Sample Organization Chart.

the way we draw organization charts. The typical organization chart tends to present a deceptively simple picture of the nature of the relationship each manager maintains with the rest of the organization. Figure 8–1 shows an organization chart that might be fairly typical of a medium-sized manufacturing company.

Assume for a moment that you are the marketing manager in Product Line B of this hypothetical manufacturing company. Although not shown on the chart, we can assume you have a sales force and maybe a market analyst and one or two other staff people reporting to you. According to the chart, you report directly to the product line manager. And that's about it. At least according to the chart that's about it. It is easy to get the impression that if you, as marketing manager in Product Line B, wanted to make a decision regarding your area of responsibility that the only interfaces you need worry about are the verticle ones—those above and below you—since those are the only relationships drawn on the chart. This would be a little naive, you say, because any good marketing manager would know that his or her decisions are bound to have some effect on the other managers in the product line. These include the manufacturing, customer service, and engineering group, *and* the managers of the other product lines. Although I must say here that even though this seems obvious to most managers, I'm amazed at the number I've encountered who don't appear to be acting as though this is obvious to them.

Thus it is easy to see that the interactions a manager has with the rest of the organization are not just one-dimensional along the verticle, as follows,

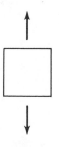

but relate to both the verticle and the horizontal.

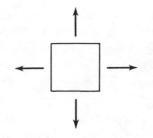

But what is not so easy for many managers to take into account is that there are still many more dimensions to every manager's interactions. For example the manager's actions could affect the world of quality assurance, finance, and material, to name a few. Thus rather than look like this,

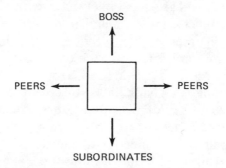

the managers' lines of interaction might be more accurately drawn like this:

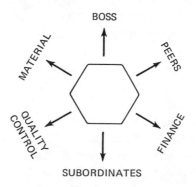

Although these lines and interfaces do not represent formal lines of authority, they do illustrate a number of different interactive dimensions. The actions of the manager could cause a number of different things (good and bad) to happen in all these different areas. Say, for example, that you, as marketing manager decide to either increase or decrease sales by 25% during the next three months. This must have some effect on almost every department in the organization. If your product line is one of the larger product lines in the company, the effect will be substantial.

But this is not all. Up to this point we've only looked at the interaction dimensions that occur within the organization. We've drawn them all on the same plane, and although there are a lot of them they are relatively easy to comprehend and to take into account. But there are many interaction dimensions that occur outside the organization as well. Your decisions will also most likely have some effect on the competition, your customers, and suppliers, to name several. Again, these effects may be slight or relatively substantial. But almost every decision you make will have some effect in each of these dimensions. Rather than picture your position as a square with four interfaces, or even as a polygon with multiple sides lying flat on one plane, it is much more accurate to visualize a three-dimensional figure. A cube is inadequate because it has too few faces to be representative. When I was in high school we had a ball, about a meter in diameter, that had been covered with little pieces of mirror glued all over the outside. At dances and parties we would hang the mirror from the ceiling and rotate it. As it rotated, light would strike all the different mirrors and reflect dozens of different rays in different directions, creating an ever-changing effect throughout the room. The interaction this multifaceted globe had with its environment comes as close as anything I can think of to describe the relationship a manager has with the managerial environment. First off there are not just one or two dimensions to the relationship as an organization chart would imply. There are dozens of interaction interfaces, each having its own orientation and direction of focus, like the mirrors on the globe. Second, every time the manager makes a move, an effect occurs along every dimension. All these effects are not bad, nor are they all good. In fact, some of them won't even matter in the overall scheme of things. However, none should be discounted or ignored until the determination has been made that they need not be worried about.

This is where troubleshooting enters into the picture. The purpose of troubleshooting is to expand the focus of thinking from the specific parameters within which the decision, problem, or course of action has been considered thus far, and to include all the possible areas that could be affected when the selected action is taken. It is important that this expanded thinking take opportunity into consideration as well as potential problems. A shortcoming in the word troubleshooting is that it implies we should address only potential "troubles" or problems. This is not true. When troubleshooting, it is equally important to search for new opportunities that may arise as a result of the intended actions.

Unfortunately, the phrase "opportunity shooting" doesn't exist. But an example of this positively oriented version of troubleshooting occurred in one of my client companies this past year. The client is a manufacturing company located in a small town in the west. The company has been growing rapidly for the past seven years. Recent volume increases on one of their production lines created serious problems with some of the equipment on the line. The problem was a result of the higher volume. At low volumes the equipment worked flawlessly and the line flowed smoothly. At the new higher volumes production became a nightmare. Newer equipment that could easily handle the higher volumes was available for purchase, but the manufacturing manager wanted to delay buying it until the following year when volumes would increase even more, making the new equipment an absolute necessity. He was also concerned about disposing of the old equipment. The new equipment was reasonably priced and a lot better in quality than the older equipment, so anyone in the market interested in buying this type of equipment would surely buy new. The manufacturing manager had a hang-up about scrapping a good piece of equipment. However, the decision was made to go ahead and purchase the new high-volume equipment to replace that which was on the line. While troubleshooting the decision, one of the managers started thinking about the old equipment. He was dissatisfied with a proposal to store it so it would be available as backup in case problems should arise with the new equipment. Storing it would be costly and the likelihood of using it in place of the new equipment was slim. However, the manager had a brother-in-law who taught at a nonprofit vocational school nearby. The school was always in need of different kinds of equipment to use in training their students. In fact, the manufacturing company frequently hired graduates of the vocational school to work in the plant. At the manager's suggestion, the company donated the old equipment to the school, and gained the following: (1) The donation became a tax deduction to the company, making the deal attractive financially; (2) the event was written up in the local newspaper and reported on a local news program, giving the company excellent public relations exposure; (3) the school changed some of its curriculum to be more in line with the employment needs of the company so all subsequent new hires that came from the school were much better prepared to work for the company; and (4) a new source of sales opened up as a result of another company's buyer reading the article. All of these tangential opportunities would have been missed completely had it not been for the troubleshooting activity. Always look for positive advantages, as well as potential problems when troubleshooting.

TROUBLESHOOTING IN EVERYDAY MANAGEMENT

At the beginning of the chapter it was stated that troubleshooting should be introduced into a manager's practices in two places. Until now we've talked about the benefit of having a segment of activity during problem-solving and decision-making activity devoted to troubleshooting. But it is also important for a manager to make a habit of conducting ongoing troubleshooting in the form of continuous critical thinking.

Albert Einstein, one of the truly great analytical thinkers and problem solvers in history, was frequently asked about his origins and the source of his genius. In a number of ways at different times he denied having any special attributes. Perhaps the best expression of his sentiments is stated in a letter he wrote to one of his close friends. He said,

> . . . Moreover, I know quite certainly that I myself have no special gift. Curiosity obsession, and dogged endurance combined with self-critique have brought me my ideas.

But the concept of self-critique is not unique to Albert Einstein. Managers and management experts have long extolled the virtues of this valuable trait. Alfred P. Sloan (of General Motors fame), Theodore N. Vail (most responsible for the Bell System's success), Peter F. Drucker, and C. Northcote Parkinson are but a few.

Critical thinking means being constantly alert for potential problems while simultaneously seeking opportunities to improve. Improvements should be sought in both method and outcomes. One of the most profound examples of productive critical thinking at the corporate level in the past hundred years is Sears, Roebuck & Company. Much of their success, which has been truly phenomenal by any business standards, can be attributed to a number of key strategy decisions that resulted from critical thinking. It was widely held "common sense" at the beginning of this century that it would be suicidal for a retailer to guarantee satisfaction or a refund. Twenty-five years later it was accepted common sense that the consumer market was too segmented for one large retailer to succeed on a nationwide scale. And twenty-five years later Sears successfully challenged the concept that retailers could only survive if they were located "downtown." They introduced the U.S. consumer to shopping centers and changed the shopping habits of America. Twenty years after that they were the first to introduce point-of-sale computers into the retail industry. To accomplish this they had to fight the entire cash register industry and buy a company that would design what Sears wanted. In the process they almost caused National Cash Register to go bankrupt. Fortunately, they learned their lesson before it was too late. In each of these cases, and many more that stand out in the history of Sears, the common denominator is proactive critical thinking. Sears management challenged the status quo and proactively sought opportunities to improve.

GENERAL PRINCIPLES FOR TROUBLESHOOTING

Regardless of strategy, there are several principles for troubleshooting that should be applied in all troubleshooting situations. First is the Principle of Occam's Razor.

OCCAM'S RAZOR

The Principle of Occam's Razor, also known as the Law of Parsimony, derived its name from William of Occam, and was originally applied as a test of scientific method. It is often stated: given two alternative explanations or descriptions, the simpler one is to be preferred, and all that is unnecessary should be ignored. In management, Occam's Razor is used a bit more proactively in troubleshooting situations to shave

away all the unnecessary trappings, leaving only the necessary ingredients for achieving the desired results. Every element of the action
plan should be reviewed in the context of the stated objectives. Any action or element that does not contain a clear relationship with the
desired outcomes should be eliminated. All the frills should be done
away with, leaving the most economical plan possible. Every action
plan, regardless of the troubleshooting strategy subsequently used,
should first of all be subjected to Occam's Razor.

PRINCIPLE OF CRITICAL REVIEW

The second principle is The Principle of Critical Review. Once again,
each action plan that is developed should be subjected to the following
analysis regardless of strategy. The action plan should be analyzed in
depth using the following questions:

1. Are the objectives of the plan sound, desirable, and
   understood?
2. What is the likelihood (or probability) the proposed course of
   action will achieve the objectives?
3. Are staffing plans adequate to carry out the action?
4. Have plans been made to capitalize on collateral advantages?
   (What other benefits might be accrued from the implementation
   of this plan?)
5. Is the plan to communicate detailed enough so that support will
   be generated and all those affected will know what to expect?
6. What are the disadvantages of the proposed action?
7. In what ways can the course of action fail?
8. Who might want to see it fail?
9. Is the proposed course of action likely to embarrass anyone such
   as top management, another department, or customers?
10. Why do anything at all? Why do this?
11. Is the time frame realistic and feasible?
12. Is there a better time to act?
13. Are there special conditions that may have been overlooked that
    could throw the project off schedule?
14. Why do it this way? Can you think of a better way?
15. Who else should give approval or be informed of the decision?

16. Is the course of action truly cost effective? If you were spending your own money is this how you would spend it?
17. Does anything about the proposed course of action make you feel at all uneasy or uncomfortable?

If these questions are asked routinely for all the plans that you as a manager are asked to review and approve, you will probably be able to eliminate somewhere between 25 and 40% of the problems that would be encountered if this step were omitted.

ABILITY TO PREDICT AND MANIPULATE THE FUTURE

The final general principle regarding troubleshooting deals with our ability to both predict and manipulate future events. No one can predict for certain any exact future occurrence. However, based on our understanding of the past and the present, it is possible to formulate some fairly detailed and reasonably reliable predictions about things that are likely to occur. And, of course, by doing certain things today it is possible for us to increase or decrease the likelihood of certain future events. If this were not true, it would be meaningless for us to accept jobs as managers, and indeed, carried further, most of what we do in life would be meaningless. But that train of thought is carrying things in the wrong direction, as it does for many people. For us, the most important line of thinking is the one that takes us into the future on the right track. And that track is one that operates on the belief that we should do more than make plans and hope they come true. Instead we should make plans and do everything possible to make them come true. As managers we must be aggressive in identifying, analyzing, and dealing with every possible factor that could have an effect on the results we intend to achieve. Several different strategies can help to accomplish this.

STRATEGIES FOR TROUBLESHOOTING

Troubleshooting means to predict problems and opportunities that are likely to occur when action is taken and to identify actions that can be taken to either avoid the problems or minimize their effects, or to capitalize on the opportunities and maximize their effects. Several strategies represent viable approaches to accomplish this. They include: (1) Predict, (2) Test, (3) Exemplify, and (4) Exaggerate. They can be used as follows.

Predict

To predict simply means to estimate as best as possible the most likely consequences of the actions being planned, then to adjust the plan accordingly to reduce the possibility of adverse outcomes and to increase the probability of positive results.

Many of the factors regarding the ability to reconstruct remote events that were described in Chapter 2 also apply here. Rather than reconstructing an event that occurred in the past, however, the goal is to project events and circumstances forward in time to create as accurate a picture as possible of what events are likely to be like at that time. The more specific the picture that is created, the more effective you will be in troubleshooting. Several methods will help increase your effectiveness at constructing a picture of future events.

Pick a specific time in the future that is relevant to your objectives, and imagine yourself at that time. What is likely to be going on in your organization? What problems will you most likely be confronting? What events will have occurred in your sphere of influence that are likely to have had an effect on your objectives and the actions you intend to carry out?

Look at basic changes that might occur in the time you will be carrying out your intended actions. Will the assumptions you've made about your operating environment still be valid? Will working conditions or characteristics of your work force have changed in ways that could have an effect on your intended action? For example, your company might be in the process of negotiating a new union contract. If a new contract takes effect prior to the completion of your plans, it is likely that your pay scales could change dramatically, thus changing your entire cost structure for the actions planned. Worse yet, it could impact the basic structure of your work force. What assumptions have you made about the economy? Will major developments in other parts of the company or the marketplace have an effect on events? What about outside forces that could cause problems, such as changes in government regulations, or pressures from stockholders?

Conduct an audit of special events that are scheduled or likely to occur in the foreseeable future. Ask what might happen at some of these special events that could cause you problems or present new opportunities. How likely are these occurrences?

Once all these have been assessed, brainstorm a list of statements that describe your situation as clearly as you can. Use these statements to create a vivid picture of what things are likely to be like in the future. Then identify the factors that are most important to address. These will be the things that are most likely to have an effect on your plan. Next decide what you should do about them. Your actions in this regard will fall into one of two categories. They will be either proactive actions, designed to increase or decrease the probability of certain things occurring, or they will be reactive actions, designed to respond to certain events should they occur. The chart in Figure 8–2 can be used to list, evaluate, and analyze these different events and actions. The first column is for listing potential problems and opportunities. The second is to provide some indication of the likelihood that the listed problem or opportunity will occur. The third column is to be used to give some indication of the level of importance or value for a given item. Proactive actions that can be taken to increase the probability of occurrence can be listed in the fourth column. The final column is for listing possible contingency plans or reactive actions to take in case the event listed in the first column does transpire. These actions should be employed most typically in the type of instance where the likely event listed in the first column was not of major importance, and perhaps unpredictable. However, it could become important if it happened, so it is wise to be prepared for it.

Test

The Test Strategy is to actually test the proposed course of action through the use of models, controlled conditions, or a representative sample, under conditions that are not too costly or time consuming. Test results can then be extrapolated to the total area that will be influenced by the intended actions. In this way fairly reliable determinations can be made regarding feasibility and potential problems.

Testing is commonly used to determine feasibility of new technology and in assessing marketing decisions. When used, however, great care must be taken that the data is used with integrity. In other words, tests should be used in decision making or troubleshooting only if they test

WHAT PROBLEMS OR OPPORTUNITIES ARE LIKELY TO OCCUR?	HOW LIKELY IS IT?	HOW IMPORTANT IS IT?	LIST OF PROACTIVE ACTIONS	LIST OF REACTIVE ACTIONS

FIGURE 8-2.   Chart for Predicting Problems and Opportunities.

the variables that are being considered. Only those factors that have been tested should be considered as reliable for use in the actual implementation of the plan. The following example from the fast-food industry illustrates how tests can backfire if this rule is violated.

A fast-food chain specializing in hamburgers decided to test the expansion of their product line by introducing a steak sandwich in some of their restaurants. During the test they included with each sandwich a small packet of steak sauce with an established brand name and proven popularity. The tests showed the steak sandwich to be extremely popular and it significantly boosted the sales volume in each restaurant. The test results were then reported to top management so the decision could be made to implement the sales of steak sandwiches nationwide. In reviewing the proposal, the chief operating officer noticed that the cost of the steak sauce that was included with each sandwich was relatively high. It wasn't so high as to make the sandwich unprofitable, but it was high enough to raise the question as to whether or not the food chain could make their own at a lower cost and thus make the steak sandwich even more profitable. They found out they could make a fairly similar sauce at a much lower cost. Thinking that the sandwich itself mattered more than the sauce, the decision was made to introduce the steak sandwich throughout the entire chain using the internally manufactured steak sauce instead of the brand that had been used in the test. The results were disastrous. In every restaurant, the pattern was the same. Overall sales volume increased during the first month the sandwich was introduced, then it dropped dramatically, in many cases to levels even lower than they were before the new product was offered. In a panic, the company went back and began new tests to isolate the problem and discovered that the problem was the steak sauce. People just didn't like it, and their level of dislike was sufficient to scare them away. The most unfortunate result, however, was that it was really too late to do much about it. Significant damage had already been suffered.

When using tests, limit the number of factors being tested. Don't test one thing and implement another. If a number of things justify testing, then test them one at a time. Most important, don't overlook the small details. Everything counts.

Exemplify

Exemplify is different from testing in that it is applied in situations or under circumstances where actual simulations or samples are not possible. Exemplify means to envision or portray different specific examples of situations that are likely to be encountered when carrying out the intended course of action, and then to analyze them in detail to identify pitfalls and problems, as well as opportunities before implementing your course of action.

Exemplify is used in circumstances when testing would be too costly in light of the benefit to be gained from the course of action, or where testing would be impractical because of the situation. For example, consider the situation where a new policy is being considered for implementation throughout the company. It would be impractical to test the policy as a strategy for troubleshooting. However it would make a great deal of sense to think of different examples of situations throughout the company where the policy might affect operations and then to think through and analyze exactly what the effects might be. For instance you might list several examples of typical work groups and ask how the new policy would work in their settings. You might ask, how would this affect the people in purchasing, finance, or personnel? Or you might think of specific operating situations that might occur and ask how the policy would help or hinder those operations.

The chief advantage of this strategy is that oftentimes we think of solutions to problems or decisions in a particular context or a very narrowly defined set of circumstances, and the use of examples forces the consideration of their effects in other situations.

Exaggerate

Quite often, issues and events can be better understood if they are blown way out of proportion for the sake of discussion or analysis. As a result, it can be helpful in many cases to deliberately exaggerate actions, events, and anticipated consequences. Hence the strategy of exaggerate, which is to deliberately overstate the events and/or consequences that are likely to occur in order to force new perspectives and deeper levels of thinking regarding the anticipated outcomes.

Worst case analysis is one of the methods that falls under the strategy of exaggerate. Worst case analysis is conducted by simply asking, "What's the worst possible thing that could happen if I do this?" More often than not, when this question is answered in detail, the answers cause the development of a new perspective regarding the issues at hand. In addition to providing new perspectives, however, this type analysis can aid substantially in generating alternatives and contingency plans for implementation in the event things do not turn out the way they are intended.

Exaggerating on the positive side has benefits too. The question should also be asked, "What will we do if things turn out to be substantially better than we predict?" Of course everything possible should be tried to help this to occur. But preparations should at least be thought through so unexpected good luck can be taken advantage of when it takes place.

By now, if all of the first five steps of the Lyles Method have been completed satisfactorily, your course of action, whether the solution to a problem or the result of your decision-making processes, should be fairly sound. All the unnecessary frills should be trimmed away, possible problems with the course of action uncovered and accounted for, and it should be ready for implementation, and above all, it should make sense to you.

However, just because it makes sense to you doesn't mean it will make sense to everyone else who might be affected or who might play a role in its ultimate success. That is why before implementation it is wise to think of communicating your plan in such a way as to gain the necessary support that will increase the probability of success. Chapter 9 presents the step of communicating, along with strategies for getting the best results from your communications effort.

9
Communicating

Overall effectiveness in problem solving and decision making is a function of both quality and acceptance. Of course the action chosen must be a good one. However, no matter how good the solution, if it is not accepted by those who must support it and act to achieve the final result, the end product will be failure. Most of the preceding chapters have dealt with issues related to developing high-quality solutions. This chapter deals with issues related to gaining acceptance for those solutions in order to achieve the optimum final results.

Before delving into the strategies of communicating, let us first review several general considerations relating to problem-solving and decision-making communication.

First must come the realization that many excellent and brilliant solutions and decisions have failed in the past because they were improperly communicated. Consistent achievers have long recognized that having a good idea, a correct solution to a problem, or a valid decision in only half the battle. All is meaningless unless it is acted upon responsibly by others.

Perhaps no one knew this as well as Albert Einstein. The history books have perhaps done a great disservice to us by not drawing enough attention to the way Einstein became famous and the manner in which he pursued recognition for and acceptance of his famous theories. We tend to look back on this great man's accomplishments and assume that he became famous and achieved notoriety because of his theories. Actually, just the opposite was true. Einstein developed most of his theories, particularly those regarding relativity, while in his teens. He quickly realized that his thinking was far from the mainstream and he would have monumental problems in trying to get serious consideration for his ideas from the established scientific community. Thus, he deliberately developed a communications strategy to gain acceptance of his ideas. At age twenty, he consciously adopted the sloppily dressed looks of an "absent-minded professor." In addition, he deliberately developed the traits of intellectual naiveté about the world of "ordinary humans," clownish playfulness, and sudden bursts of enthusiasm, which he displayed only in public. As a result, he gained attention for himself, and his ideas then gained serious consideration much sooner than they probably would have done had Einstein himself not been such a pragmatic communicator.

Good communications and transfer of understanding doesn't "just happen." Effective communication is the result of careful and deliberate planning.

In planning an effective communications strategy, the manager must not assume that others know anything at all about the decision or plan to act. In fact, to be safe, the manager should always assume that others understand even less than they appear to understand. Demonstrated awareness does not prove understanding. And even understanding is not enough to ensure the desired results. No one has demonstrated a better knowledge of this principle, nor a deeper appreciation for its use, than the marketing experts who diagrammed the thinking levels people must progress through prior to acting. These marketing experts say that in order to achieve the desired action on the part of the person for whom the communicaton is intended, they must progress through five levels of thinking. The same holds true for most management communications. The levels start with the assumption that the other person is totally unaware that you are trying to implement a course of action which makes some demand on them, and finishes with the person actually taking the desired action. It can be illustrated as follows.

UNAWARENESS
AWARENESS
UNDERSTANDING
COMMITMENT
ACTION

First of all, assume that no one else is aware of what you are trying to accomplish. You must first do something that will get their attention in a positive manner. When you have penetrated the level of unawareness, however, all you have achieved is awareness. Awareness by itself will not produce the desired result. In order to achieve responsible action, the people affected must understand what is intended and the context in which they must act. At this point, however, they may still not be motivated. The benefits to them of acting in a particular manner must also be conveyed. Commitment must be deliberately developed. And finally, there must be some triggering mechanism to cause the action to occur. Each of these levels must be carefully and methodically worked through if success is to be achieved.

Examine well-written advertising copy and you will discover elements addressing each of these levels. For example, most full-page magazine ads will have about two-thirds of the page devoted to an eye-catching and appealing picture. The purpose of this is to attract attention—to penetrate the level of unawareness and draw attention to the ad. Typically there will then be about a third of a page of text to explain the product or service being sold. This addresses the issue of understanding. If the copy is well written, the explanations will not only describe features of the product, but they will describe them in terms of benefits to the potential buyer. If there are particular advantages to a particular group of buyers, these advantages will be highlighted in order to develop as much motivation and commitment as possible. And finally, there will be a "buy today" or similar kind of directive to spur the reader to action. Although intent here is not to get all management communications to take on the appearance of slick magazine advertisements, the principles involved apply to both fields.

Consider how many times you've encountered the following type of situation. Because of the changing circumstances involved in a growing organization, a particular problem has surfaced and is continuing to recur on a rather frequent basis. An example might be in the area of purchasing, where a number of line supervisors have started using rather informal methods to procure supplies. This is causing headaches for the finance people who must account for all these expenditures and keep track of where everything is going. The entire organization comes under stress because of the sloppy procedures, so the head of the organization tells the head of the finance group to solve the problem. The finance head calls a few key people together and they work out a new policy that will eliminate the sloppy practices and give the organization the controls it needs. The finance head makes a presentation to the chief executive, who approves the policy and orders it implemented. Satisfied, and feeling a sense of accomplishment, the finance head has the policy printed up and disseminated through the normal distribution channels for written communications. And one or more of the following occur.

1. Resentment builds up among the line supervisors who feel that staff is laying more red tape and needless administrative hassles on them.
2. Some of the supervisors read the policy bulletin and throw it away.
3. Some of the supervisors do what is necessary to meet the absolute minimum requirements of the new policy.
4. Very few might try to carry the policy out to the extreme in an attempt to sandbag it.
5. Some will do what the policy asks.

The problem is that the finance head jumped from the unawareness level all the way down to the action level, ignoring the necessary considerations in between. All of the above actions that are undesirable are clearly the result of lack of understanding and lack of commitment. The finance head presumed that everyone who received the new policy would appreciate the need for the policy and the benefits for implementation. This rarely happens. No matter who is the intended target for communications, the safest assumption is that he/she is preoccupied with his/her own problems and concerns and will do little to facilitate understanding of your problems and concerns. Part of the reason for this is that most people naturally give their own job and responsibilities the highest personal priority. But part of it also is because there is a large amount of information flowing in all directions, all the time, and it is an overwhelming task for most people to sort everything out to the degree necessary to stay "on top" of things.

This raises another important point regarding any kind of communications in organizations of any size. At any time in most organizations there is a lot of background noise—information being transmitted, and less being received—that is working to clog up the communication channels and networks. To be an effective communicator the manager must organize and package the message he / she is trying to send in such a way that it stands out against this background. The degree of formality has a lot to do with whether a message will be understood and responded to.

A common complaint among managers is that the people in their particular organization are unresponsive—they don't react positively to new ideas and suggestions. In my consulting work, lower-level supervisors and middle-level managers frequently voice this complaint to me. Lately I've been responding to this complaint with questions regarding the mode of communications, and the dialogue typically turns out to sound something like this.

The manager says, "I heard all that stuff you said about being innovative and trying new solutions, but it would never work in my organization."

I respond by asking why not.

"Because nobody in top management positions in this organization every supports new ideas," the manager says. "They won't try anything new and won't even respond to people's suggestions."

"Have you proposed any new ideas recently?" I ask.

"Oh yeah, lots of them. All the time," the manager says. "I had a great one last week, but as usual, I suggested it, and nothing happened."

"Really? Who did your proposal go to and how did you send it?" I ask.

"I suggested it to my boss," says the manager, "that's who I'm supposed to send it to, I think. I mentioned it to him while he was standing in line at the cafeteria for lunch the other day. He said he appreciated the suggestion and would give it to his boss, who would have to make the final decision on it. I never heard another thing about it, just like all the good ideas I suggest."

Believe it or not, this is *not* uncommon. It is amazing how many good ideas get presented in elevators, parking lots, on the way home from work (sometimes on Friday afternoons, even), during chance meetings at the coffee pot or the drinking fountain, at cocktail parties, chance meetings in the hallway, and the like. It is even more amazing how many people are surprised that their ideas presented in these settings are not scooped up, embraced, and implemented without delay. Contrary to popular belief (and it must be popular because so many people act this way), this is *not* the way to propose a good idea, or the solution to a problem and expect it to gain favorable recognition or reaction. These *may* be acceptable settings in which to lobby for a course of action once it has been proposed, but rarely will an idea proposed this casually be acted upon to any reasonable degree.

If a proposal is to be seriously considered, it must be seriously presented. This means completing a certain amount of preparation—doing your homework. When the proposal is completed, consider asking your boss for an appointment to present the proposal, no matter how good of a working relationship you may have with your boss. This will get the boss's attention. It will cause your idea to penetrate the level of unawareness, bringing into the boss's level of awareness that you have something serious to talk about. Even though this may seem unnecessary, the message you'll communicate by asking for an appointment is, "I have something serious to discuss."

Then if you've done your homework, when you sit down with the boss to review your proposal, you'll gain still more of a favorable reaction. The boss can't help but think that because you've done so much preparation, this must be an important idea. Because of this you'll more likely communicate understanding. It is much easier to explain something to a receptive audience than an audience that is simultaneously dealing with several other issues. Ideally, as part of your preparation you will have built a camel (see page 25 in Chapter 2, for instruction on how to build a camel). This will have allowed you to integrate the goals of your proposal with top priority goals of your boss and anyone else who will be involved. This is one sure way of gaining commitment to your proposal, although it is not the only way. The benefits of your idea must be communicated in terms that are meaningful to the person you are addressing. No matter how good your idea is, if the person you are proposing it to doesn't see some personal benefits in its implementation, your odds of success will correspondingly lower. Remember, benefit exists in the eyes of the beholder. You may have what appears to be the best idea in the world to you, but if others do not perceive the same benefit, then there is no way it can become the best. Remember the following:

> When communicating an idea, whether it is a decision you are attempting to implement, a solution to one of your problems, or something innovative you'd like to see implemented,

1. Do your homework—prepare so the idea can be communicated in a detailed and hard-hitting presentation.
2. Present the idea formally, no matter who you are presenting to and how informal your relationship with that person might be.
3. Ensure there are some benefits to the recipient of your proposal that are likely to cause the recipient to be motivated to respond favorably *and* help carry out the intended course of action.
4. Don't violate the lines of authority, but make sure your plan to communicate will carry your proposal to *all* those who will have a say in approving your idea.

ONE-WAY COMMUNICATIONS IS INEFFECTIVE

There is no such thing as effective one-way communications. To be effective, communications must travel in both directions between sender and receiver. There must be feedback that the initial message was received and understood in the context that was intended. Thus any plan for communicating must contain a mechanism for feedback and testing in order for the person who sent the message to be able to know exactly what effect the message had.

Figures 9–1 and 9–2 contain formats for you to use in planning your communications relative to the action plans you develop. They should be used regardless of strategy.

STRATEGIES FOR COMMUNICATING

Once you have planned who and what needs to be communicated, you should choose your strategy from one of the following: (1) Write, (2) Verbalize, (3) Promote, or (4) Symbolize. Choosing the right strategy should depend to a large extent on the type of effect you want to create and the extent to which support is needed for the accomplishment of your objectives.

PLAN TO COMMUNICATE

Who will be affected by this action? How will they be affected?

_____

_____

_____

Who do we need support from for success? What type of support?

_____

_____

_____

What benefits can be identified that will accrue to those affected and to those whose support is needed for successful implementation? Be sure the benefits identified are benefits they perceive.

To those affected?   To those whose support is needed?

_____   _____

_____   _____

_____   _____

_____   _____

_____   _____

_____   _____

_____   _____

_____   _____

How will you test the effectiveness of your communications?

_____

_____

_____

_____

Now complete the plan by filling in the form on the following page.

FIGURE 9-1. Page One of Plan to Communicate.

Write

To write, as a strategy, means to inform through a written format such as a memorandum, letter, telegram, policy bulletin, internal house organ, or other publication. It is a formal strategy and is usually used when specificity and documentation are important.

COMMUNICATIONS TARGET (Either a person or a population)	PRIORITY	TARGET OBJECTIVE (What I want as a result)	MODE	BY WHEN

FIGURE 9-2. Page Two of Plan to Communicate.

Good writing is distinguished by several characteristics. First of all, it should get the job done exactly the way it is intended. That is to say, it should not require further explanation—no meetings should be required to study instructions or intent, and no more letters should be required asking for more information. Any written communications should be clear and complete, leaving no doubt or confusion. And finally, good writing does not take unfair advantage of a "captive" audience. Just because subordinates and others in the organization are required to read your writing is no reason for giving them anything but the best.

Writing simple language in a clear, concise manner is not easy; there are not shortcuts for success in writing. But every manager can and should learn to write plainly and simply. It will take practice and self-critique. But the results, in terms of achieving results and preventing more problems from occurring, will be worth it. Here are a few simple rules to help you improve the effectiveness of your writing.

1. *Know your readers and write to their interests and their level.* Earlier in this chapter we talked about developing commitment by addressing benefits to the receivers of your communications. Here we are expanding this concept to include factors other than benefits. Rarely will you be trying to influence a completely homogeneous group of people. Writing to technical people will be different from writing to laborers.

2. *Plan your writing.* Earlier we talked about planning your overall communications effort and provided a Plan to Communicate in Figures 9–1 and 9–2. The Plan to Communicate is different from planning what you are going to write. Now it is time to prepare an outline of the topic in question. If you plan on dictating your message, it is essential to organize your thoughts in advance. Arrange your subject matter in a logical way. Don't make the reader jump back and forth to understand what you are saying. After completing the outline, check to see that everything has been included.

3. *Write simply.* Avoid complex and compound-complex sentences. When you can use a simple term or sentence in the place of a difficult one, use it. Study newspapers and use a similar style of writing.

4. *Keep Sentences and Paragraphs Short.* Sentences should average no more than eighteen words in length. Of course, you will want to vary the length of both paragraphs and sentences, but the average length should be reasonably short. To check your writing, select something you have written. Count all the words and the number of sentences. Then divide the number of words in the sample by the number of sentences. The following table will give an indication of how difficult your writing is to read.

Average Sentence Length	Level Of Writing
10 words or less	Very easy
12	Easy
14	Fairly easy
17	Standard
21	Fairly difficult
25 words or less	Difficult
29 or more	Very difficult

Using several samples will give the best picture of your true level of writing.

5. *Enlarge your vocabulary of plain words.* Emphasis here is on the word plain. The goal is to become flexible without becoming obscure. Use a dictionary or thesaurus to select short, simple synonyms. Use short, concrete words that your readers can visualize. Avoid abstract terms and uncommon words that make your readers work to get your message.

6. *Avoid unnecessary words.* Don't use unnecessary words to "dress up" your writing. Make each word count. Never annoy your readers by making them wade through a lot of necessary words to understand your intended meaning.

7. *Use action verbs rather than passive verbs whenever possible.* Use strong, active verbs rather than passive verbs. "We will sell" is stronger than "We will be selling." Don't use verbs that have "ing" as a suffix (present participle). Use active rather than passive voice, and make the message as personal as possible.

8. *Use Examples to Add Meaning to Your Message.* Quite often examples help to show exactly how your proposal will work. Many people understand concepts best when they can see how they are applied in real life situations. Examples help make intangible principles concrete and therefore more easily understood.

9. *Use Visual Aids.* Exhibits, such as drawings, charts, tables, graphs, and pictures will help you make your point. Often they can show relationships and provide comparisons more clearly and simply than the written word alone.

When your writing is completed, proofread and edit it. If you can get others to read and comment on your work, take the time to do so.

Many people find it particularly useful to let something they have written sit for a few days before they review it again and give it a final proofreading. Often when we write something, the ideas are so clear in our own minds that we naturally assume the same clarity is being transferred to paper. A two-day seasoning period allows us to come back to the written document with a fresh approach. If the same clarity can be developed on paper as exists mentally, then the message will probably come across fairly clearly to the people for whom it was written.

VERBALIZE

Oftentimes it is better to explain things orally, either via telephone, in person, through electronic media such as television or videotape, or in the form of a public presentation or address. The advantage of oral communication is that the information thus conveyed tends to be more personal, and there is an increased opportunity to project true feeling and intent. If the medium employed is the telephone or one that allows for interaction, then the opportunities for questions and feedback will be increased.

Many of the same rules apply to oral communications as apply to those conveyed in writing. Your message should be thought out in advance, the audience analyzed, your actual presentation prepared and critiqued, and your objectives fairly clearly specified. Opportunities for questioning should be provided, either periodically during the presentation or at the end. Feedback should be solicited. Always ask, "What did you understand?" rather than, "Did you understand?" Most important, remember that the very best communicators continually listen while they are talking. They listen to everything that is going on around them and are particularly sensitive to any clues that might indicate how well they are being received.

Visual aids should be considered when making oral presentations also. They can serve to focus the conversation and keep any discussions that might arise on track. Often in conversations it is difficult to keep discussion on the topics intended. A picture, table, chart, or written agenda can help immensely in this area.

Timing is another critical factor to consider when communicating verbally. Pick a time and location for your conversation or presentation when distractions will be kept to a minimum. Because the average person speaks at rate of 100 to 125 words per minute and the average person thinks at a rate of 400 to 500 words per minute, we all have a tendency to allow our attention to wander when we are listening to someone else speak. Take this into account and set up your meetings when people have the time to spend, and hold them in a place where there will be little opportunity for outside distractions and interference.

At the end of your discussion period always summarize the key points. List any decisions that you have agreed upon and review any expectations that might be laid out for the future. Check one final time to make sure the key points in your discussion are agreed upon and understood.

PROMOTE

To promote is to creatively induce information to be passed along by sparking interest or enthusiasm among those who will be affected in order that they will be motivated to tell others and have those others pass along the interest and enthusiasm in their turn. Advertisements, contests, and the like are often good ways to communicate new policies and procedures to employees so they will respond with a positive attitude.

A good example of this strategy in action is the approach many companies use when personnel recruitment becomes a problem in tight employment markets. Rather than merely tell all the employees that the company is in dire need of new employees, the company will offer rewards and incentives for their current employees to recruit good people. Some campaigns that I have observed, and considered to be quite effective have offered color televisions, savings bonds, or cash bonuses to employees who introduce a person who is subsequently hired by the company. In order for the current employees to persuade others to take an interest in the company they must first become very familiar with all the benefits and advantages that go along with their own jobs. This type of campaign helps to get the word on the street that the company is hiring much more quickly than it would normally be communicated using traditional advertising methods.

The important point to remember is that reward systems and incentives can be manipulated to generate excitement regarding certain issues that are important to management of the company. Safety campaigns are often used to create a much higher level of awareness regarding safety issues and procedures than might otherwise occur if safety procedures were merely published in a policy bulletin or safety handbook. A prize awarded to the person who devises the most clever safety cartoon or slogan can often generate a much higher level of awareness than otherwise might occur.

An advantage of these kinds of promotional techniques is that they help to create an organizational environment that is more alive and interesting than it would otherwise be. Some organizations try to make it a point to always have something going on just to stimulate the thinking and general level of attentiveness of their employees. The informal grapevine is always going to be working in an organization of any size, whether you like it or not, so why not let it work for you, in support of organizational goals, rather than in some other direction?

SYMBOLIZE

The world of communication is rapidly becoming a collage of symbols. Traveling has been made more convenient and comfortable during the recent past by the adoption of a set of international symbols that signal the presence of restaurants, rest rooms, smoking and nonsmoking areas, taxi stands, bus stops, throughfares, and the like. In many cases the message you are trying to convey can be better illustrated through pictures, drawings, diagrams, charts, murals, or graphs, then through words, either written or spoken. Not only does the message oftentimes get communicated much more clearly, but a properly placed sign or symbol can provide low-key reinforcement on an ongoing basis that might not be attainable through the use of any other method.

Another advantage is that symbolizing tends to force simplification. There can be no doubt that as our world naturally becomes more complicated and complex, any attempt to simplify things, particularly in the area of communication must be worthwhile. Certainly it will be appreciated by those for whom the communication is intended.

Certainly we know that symbols, tables, charts, pictograms, drawings, and sketches are not new devices for communicating ideas. Throughout the world we have discovered symbolic representations on cave walls, buildings, and in ancient documents. Many of these symbols communicate their messages through time at least as effectively as words could have done. Some people think they have been even more effective because they capture mood and perspective in ways that would not have been possible with words.

Perhaps the most common method of symbolizing in management occurs in the use of graphs and charts. Complex relationships between different variables such as sales, volume, sums of money, and how different factors affect them are frequently much more easily understood when charted or graphed. The same can be said of many working rela-

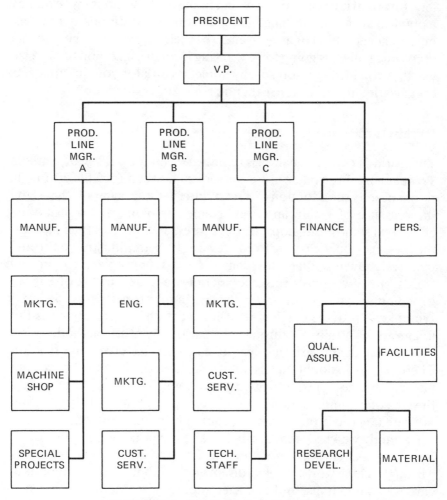

FIGURE 9–3. Sample Organization Chart.

tionships between people. For example, try to imagine how much more difficult it would be to describe the organization chart pictured in Figure 9–3 in narrative form than it is to describe it in the format presented. It would be frivolous to argue that written descriptions could communicate the reporting relationships and general responsibilities of everyone as quickly and clearly as the chart does.

Another common example of symbols being used very effectively is flow charts. Flow charts indicate the direction of movement of a product or a process from the initial stages to completion. Blocks with words or pictures in them are used to depict different stages in the process, and arrows are drawn between the different blocks to indicate the flow of work from one stage of the process to the next. Frequently the work on an assembly line is laid out symbolically like this so new employees can learn the flow quickly and easily and understand how their particular work fits in with the total line's effort. Routing diagrams are often laid out in a very similar manner so that approval processes for requests and the like can be tracked and understood.

Oftentimes decision-making processes can be communicated more effectively through the use of symbols and charts. For example, M. Wayne Wilson, developed the decision tree in Figure 9–4 for Inter-North while serving as Director of Corporate Staff Organization Development and Training, to help managers think through the training decisions they are required to make regarding the development of individual subordinates.

Drawings, photographs, and illustrations are all additional ways to communicate symbolically. The use of these items has increased dramatically in the past few years as people become more adept in their use and the effects of their use become more apparent. The bottom line is one of creativity combined with total impact. To be effective as a communicator in this day and age requires both. With this thought in mind it is worth trying to develop and use communication strategies that avoid placing total dependence on words to get the message across.

Now that your efforts at communicating have paved the way for your actions, it is time to act. Chapter 10 will focus on the process of implementation which is the focal point of all our previous efforts. All that has been discussed up until now is meaningless if the final results are not achieved.

TRAINING METHOD DECISION TREE

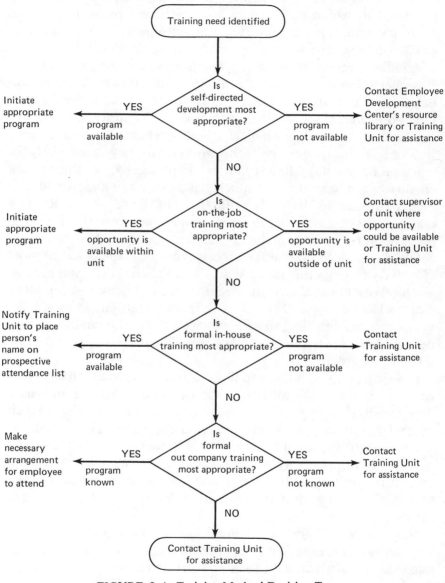

FIGURE 9–4. Training Method Decision Tree.

10
Implementing

One of my most memorable lessons in management occurred early in my career. I had been working long and hard on a special project for my boss. My overriding concern was to prove that I really "knew my stuff," and to show my boss the quality of work I was capable of. In the process all my attention gradually turned inward. I failed to realize that things were happening elsewhere that would have an adverse effect on the results of my project. To some extent, I guess I even went so far as to deliberately brush aside some of these warning signals on the assumption that if I did the best I could on the project, then that would be the prevailing criterion my boss would use in evaluating my performance. Well, I did good work. The technical work I accomplished on the project was indeed masterful. Although when implemented the desired results were not achieved, I felt certain my boss would be pleased with my effort and would recognize that it was someone else's fault that everything had not turned out as intended. In fact, at one time during the project when a colleague told me about some of the things other people were doing that would interfere with my project's results, I gave a "so what" reponse saying something to the effect of, "if they can't recognize what a good thing this is, then they'll have to pay the price eventually and be embarrassed by their own ignorance."

When the project was completed, having fallen short of its mark, my boss called a meeting to critique the results. I looked forward to the meeting, assuming I would get praise for my efforts and the others would suffer their rebukes. One of the biggest surprises of my life came when the exact opposite happened. My first true lesson in management responsibility began when my boss said, "Dick, just being good won't get you into heaven—you've got to be good *for something!*" (Years later I encountered a cartoon from the medical field making a similar point. It showed a doctor walking out of the operating room exclaiming to an anxiously awaiting wife, "Great news Mrs. Jones, the operation was a success even though your husband died.") When I offered the excuse to my boss that I had done good work and the lack of results were not my fault, his response was, "there is no excuse." And, of course, he was correct. In management, if a person is assigned responsibilities, then that person alone must be held accountable for carrying them out—no excuses, and no buck passing—regardless of what others may or may not do.

If organizational performance is to be sustained, then individual managers must be assigned (or they must voluntarily acquire) specific responsibilities—without dual or joint accountability—and their performance must be assessed on the basis of whether or not the results incumbent on these responsibilities are achieved. The first level of assessment is *whether* or *not* the intended results have been achieved. The second level, which is only like the frosting on the cake, is *how well* the results were achieved. Unfortunately, many managers tend to examine accomplishment in just the reverse order. They assume results can be measured in incremental steps. Accordingly they start with the "how well" evaluation, and count any activity aimed at achieving the results as evidence of performance. This may be helpful at times, but can also be misleading.

The results that matter most are the final results—to be able to say, "yes, I accomplished the intended objectives." That is why this chapter and the concepts regarding implementation are so important. Nothing is worse than seeing an absolutely brilliant solution to a problem fail because the originator figured the battle was over as soon as the idea had been communicated.

One of the truly fatal assumptions a manager can make is that everyone else (or anyone else, for that matter) cares about the idea, is concerned about its accomplishment, or recognizes its merit. This is true even if the entire future of the organization hinges upon the plan's success. It's not that everyone else is bad or stupid. Rather it is because they all have their own priorities and suffer from a sort of "organizational tunnel vision" closely aligned with the boundaries of their individual jobs. Good managers recognize this. Rather than complain or blame others for lack of support, they do whatever is necessary, short of undermining others, to achieve the results they are on the payroll to produce.

One of the best examples of this I have ever encountered is a machine shop supervisor who works for a high-technology manufacturing company that is a client of mine. Although Barney may not be the most popular supervisor in the plant, his straightforward, outspoken, and colorful style have earned him the respect of just about everyone. He has a widespread reputation that, no matter what, Barney will get the job done. Period. He does what it takes regardless of circumstance. One example occurred during a period of extremely rapid growth for the plant. The personnel department and the purchasing department were swamped with work. The line departments couldn't hire people fast enough to meet the demands of the expansion, and the purchasing department was processing three times the number of purchase orders they had been handling just a few months earlier. Everyone was blaming everyone else for their own inability to accomplish what they were supposed to. Everyone that is, except Barney. Not once did he utter the words "I couldn't do it because personnel didn't find enough good people for me." Nor did he ever ask, "How can I make something when I don't have the materials and parts I need?" He didn't have to. Barney saw the big picture and realized that if he was going to continue to succeed, he would have to do things he normally didn't do. They weren't complicated or mysterious things, but they were different and they worked. The most noticeable was that each morning immediately after his people had settled in he would "make the rounds." First he went to the personnel manager's office to review progress on all his job orders and discuss recruiting strategy. While just about everyone else in the plant was submitting job orders then not doing anything else until they felt it was time to complain or make excuses, Barney was getting his positions filled. His next stop each morning was purchasing, where the same thing happened. While others complained, Barney got the job done, because he operates on the philosophy that once a person agrees to do something, it is up to that person to do it, even if it means going outside the system occasionally, which he's not afraid to do. Most of the time, however, he works within the system to get what he wants.

Barney's attitude about the organization, its rules, regulations, and demands is also worth noting. Like many other managers, Barney frequently locks horns with policies or regulations that interfere with the accomplishment of his short-term objectives. If he doesn't understand why these rules exist, he'll very aggressively question them. If they are invalid or obsolete, he'll accept it as his own personal responsibility to see to it they are amended properly or eliminated. If they are found to be needed for some reason, then he will make every effort to work within their boundaries when implementing his action plans. If he can't accomplish this, then he'll work around them, making as little fuss as possible in the process. One thing he will never do, however, is to whine or complain about them. No one has ever heard Barney say "this system is all screwed up around here," or "this company does things all wrong." When it comes to rules, regulations, the system, and management, Barney doesn't think in terms of good or bad, right or wrong. He doesn't get caught up in the practice of assessing all his actions to be good and anything that interferes with him as bad. He knows that conflict is inevitable in organizations. It is inevitable because of the large number of people in different roles and the large number of things to be done. This is not bad. It just is. And that is exactly how Barney treats the situation. He treats certain situations as "givens." The circumstances are given conditions within which he must operate. Such constraints exist in all organizations. They are a price we must pay in order to be able to reap the rewards of organizational endeavor. Once they are established and validated for some purpose, nothing can be gained by grousing and griping. The wise manager, like Barney, will recognize the benefits of channeling energy toward accomplishment instead.

GUIDELINES FOR SUCCESSFUL IMPLEMENTATION

Implementation means to cause changes to occur somewhere in your sphere of influence as a manager. It is impossible to implement any course of action and not have something change as a result. This means that certain things must be disrupted or discontinued and new activities must begin. But most important, it means that after you have initiated action, things will be different. This makes so much sense, but it is all too often overlooked by a good many managers. The oversight is reflected in comments such as, "Well let's do it, but be careful not to make any waves." Or they might say something like, "Let's get this done with as little effect as possible." One of the most interesting I've encountered occurs often when scheduling managment training programs. The inexperienced and naive people in charge of setting up such programs will tip off their lack of depth by saying something like, "Okay, now that we've designed the program we're going to offer let's schedule it so as to have the minimum amount of disruption possible." This seems to me to be less than effective if what you're trying to do is disrupt old behavior patterns and cause people to do things differently. You simply can't expect people to change when you are asking them not to. There is a certain amount of disruptiveness that must accompany any changes. This is not bad, it is just a fact of life. The key is in creating exactly the right amount of disruption. The following guidelines should help to accomplish successful implementation of your action plan with the minimum amount of adverse disruption and the maximum amount of success.

1. *Always implement changes from the top down.* Changes in organizations do not flow up. A common mistake among upper-level managers is to assume that they can do without whatever is being implemented, and the most important and valuable results will be realized if action is first taken at the bottom levels of supervision or among the workforce. This rarely turns out to be the case. The most effective changes take place when the environment has been established that will nurture and support the desired behaviors and activities. This can only be accomplished if the people in policy-making and key operating positions are on board first.

2. *Always start with the best first.* Build on strengths, not weaknesses. If given a choice between implementing a new idea in a really good work group and one that is struggling along, do it first with the good group. Several reasons justify this. First, it is important that your early results are as positive as possible. Failure off the starting line could doom the entire plan to defeat. Second, you should always attempt to position your best people on the leading edge. The people in your organization should be conditioned to follow winners, not losers. Third, they have earned the opportunity to be innovative. There aren't many ways to reward good people that are better than letting them be the pioneers.

3. *Set your own example.* Nothing is more convincing than to see someone doing exactly what they are asking others to do. Nothing will

establish new norms more quickly than for the leaders in the organization to start behaving in the desired manner themselves. Quite often, as part of a strategy for implementation, a manager will change his or her own behavior in a certain way several days, or even weeks before asking others to do the same. This lends a certain credibility to the request that might be lacking with any other approach.

4. *Remember that you can't motivate people to do something they don't know how to do.* Base level knowledge and ability are oftentimes the overlooked factor that dooms many good plans to failure. Ensure that if specialized knowledge or skills that do not already exist are required for the success of your plan, that opportunities to acquire them are provided during your implementation process. Resources to consider include, public seminars, in-house seminars, in-house presentations, informal discussion groups, audio or videotape recordings, or self-teaching materials. Whatever, the mode, however, the important factor is to make sure people have the basic ability to do what you ask them to do.

5. *Recognize and reward desired performance early.* People should do what is expected. If you have communicated in terms that have conveyed benefit to them that is meaningful to them, they should be fairly motivated as a matter of course. However, the overall level of performance, and the level at which the performance is sustained, can be dramatically affected if people are recognized for doing the right things and are rewarded in a manner that is meaningful to them. Any time people do something new, everyone is looking for some signal from the organization or from management that will indicate to them the extent to which the new behaviors or actions are valued. A clear and forceful message as early as possible to still be meaningful can make a great deal of difference. Among other things, it will disarm the skeptics and provide additional comfort to your supporters.

6. *Pace implementation so timing is consistent with the needs of your plan.* If it takes too long to accomplish your aims, people will lose interest and choose not to take you seriously enough. On the other hand, it is possible to push too hard and build up a wall of resistance that will also prevent you from accomplishing your desired results. Each plan is different and everything you attempt will require different timing. The important thing is to be sensitive to everything else that is happening at the same time and to the reactions of those involved. Make sure things happen at a brisk pace, quickly enough to keep up interest and enthusiasm, but not so quickly as to build up resistance.

7. *Provide coaching and follow-up consulting, and most of all, be persistent.* Don't expect that once everyone is informed of their responsibilities and your expectations regarding their performance that everything you desire will naturally occur. Where others are involved, oftentimes the slightest problem or obstacle will give cause to abandon the effort. Minor irritations will frequently be all that is needed for someone else to give up trying completely where your action plan is concerned. In these cases, your expertise must be brought to bear to solve these minor problems and overcome the obstacles to successful implementation. But most of all you will have to be the persistent one when energy wanes.

Several key strategy options exist for implementation. They will be presented and discussed in the next section.

STRATEGIES FOR IMPLEMENTING

The final step in the Lyles Method, Implementing, means to initiate action to achieve the specified objective and to maintain the desired consequences. Four strategies for achieving effective implementation include, (1) Do It Yourself, (2) Delegate, (3) Phase-In, and (4) Systemize. They work as follows.

Do It Yourself

This means to take all the necessary actions and follow through on all activities yourself, without help and without delegating anything to subordinates. As a general rule this strategy should be avoided if at all possible. Whenever possible, Delegate is preferred over the strategy of Do It Yourself. However, there will be circumstances that justify doing it yourself. One strong reason might be that it is necessary for you to convey to others around you that you think the action you are taking is important. Assuming you don't try to do everything yourself anyway, then when you do choose to do something yourself others will take note of this and attach a greater sense of urgency to your action plan than they might if you delegated it. Another reason might be that it is important for the desired action to be carried out exactly as you want it to be. Rather than run the risk of having someone else deviate from the intended action, a sure way to ensure precision is to do it yourself. However, it should be pointed out that if you are doing a lot of things yourself because you feel this way about most things, then you are probably not taking enough risks and are probably not allowing your subordinates to grow and be challenged enough. A final reason for justifying doing something yourself is urgent time constraints. If immediate action is imperative, oftentimes doing it yourself is the most expeditious route.

The problems with doing it yourself are many. First of all, you might easily become overburdened with work and deny yourself the opportunity to be a proactive and innovative manager. Second, you are withholding responsibilities and meaningful work opportunities from your subordinates. Another reason is that you will be precluding an opportunity for additional creative input from others whom you might delegate to. Fourth, you deny the opportunity for anyone else to take ownership or accept personal responsiblity for the results you are trying to accomplish. Fifth, you minimize the opportunities for personal growth, development, and learning on the part of your subordinates. And finally, you thwart any feelings of team spirit and cohesiveness, reinforcing the attitude that you and members of your work group are better off working independently rather than as a group.

Delegate

Delegate means to direct others to accomplish the necessary tasks without your involvement. However, effective delegation is more than merely giving other people work to do. Effective delegation means making meaningful assignments to subordinates that will be both challenging and rewarding. It means giving people meaningful responsibilities for accomplishing work that is gratifying and fulfilling. The following guidelines should be helpful in delegating.

1. Make sure everyone understands exactly what has been delegated. All involved should know what they are being held accountable for and what the extent of their individual accountability is.
2. For each specific result, make sure only one person is held accountable. Joint or dual accountability is no accountability. Avoid confusion by placing individual accountability in the most appropriate place.
3. Delegate authority along with accountability and responsibility.

Nothing is more frustrating than to be asked to do something, and to be held accountable for accomplishing it, but to be denied the tools necessary for its accomplishment. Authority is often one of the tools required to get things done. Make sure it is given when necessary.

4. Specify an agreed-upon reporting system so you will know how things are progressing and whether or not any problems arise. Make sure your reporting system has some mechanism for early warning regarding potential problems so, if necessary, you can take whatever action is necessary to stave off disaster before it strikes.

5. Let all those who might be affected know exactly what has been delegated so they can be supportive and understand what is happening.

6. Assign milestones and target dates for accomplishment so everyone can assume the same degree of urgency regarding the matters under consideration.

7. Give as much freedom as possible to the people you delegate to. When possible focus on results rather than methods.

8. Make assignments in a motivating and challenging way so as to stimulate as much enthusiasm and excitement as possible. Try to avoid laying "busywork" on people.

9. As much as possible, make the assignments fit the person. Take into account knowledge, experience, career development needs, training needs, ability, and aptitude, to gain as much benefit as possible from each action that you delegate.

10. Always elicit feedback to ensure that everyone involved understands exactly what is expected.

A popular definition for the term management describes it as a process for getting things done through people. The strategy of Delegate is the most direct avenue one has for applying this process effectively.

Phase In

There will be times when action plans need to be implemented with as little disturbance as possible to everything else that is going on in the organization. When this need arises, and when the action plan is fairly comprehensive or involved, the strategy of Phase In should be considered. Phase In means to do a little at a time with short intervals between each action step. It is an integrative-type strategy that is oriented toward producing the desired result with the least amount of disturbance possible.

Phase In is used most frequently when changes are being made in one area of concern and it is important to leave other areas as undisturbed as possible. For example, assume that you have been working on an attendance problem in the production area and that your solution to the problem was to implement a completely new policy oriented toward attendance and absenteeism. However, production has been running fairly smoothly and you want to do everything possible to keep from disrupting shipments or the flow of work. Rather than enter the plant one morning and suddenly announce a broad new package of personnel policies, it might be wiser to make a few changes at a time. This will bring about the changes you desire in the primary area of concern without disrupting things in another area that, although you are concerned about it, is not something you want disrupted as a part of solving your problem.

Phase In can be used with either or both of the previous two strategies. Because it is generally used with action plans that are fairly comprehensive, you might want to consider a combination of the two. For example, you may wish to do some of the action items yourself and you may want to delegate some parts to others.

There is no magic to this rather simple strategy. However, it does require some thought and the use of anticipatory thinking to determine what should be beneficial pacing and relevant time frames.

Systemize

Simply stated, Systemize means to make something part of the system. In the context of problem solving and decision making, it means to change basic foundations, such as the organization's structure, policies, or reward systems to ensure that the desired actions are carried out properly on an ongoing basis.

Many changes in organizations frequently wither and die on the vine because they lack the necessary formal supports to sustain the desired behavior patterns and actions once they have been announced and directed. Oftentimes changes are implemented without the responsible manager ever knowing or realizing that there are existing policies and regulations that work to undermine the new changes.

Formal reward and incentive systems are good mechanisms to consider when one is trying to create permanent changes and foster support for those changes within the organization. Programs for recognizing and bringing positive attention to those who are behaving the way they are supposed to are usually very powerful forces in causing the right things to occur. Suggestion award programs have had substantially positive results in this regard. Organizations who prize innovation and improved productivity have typically established this type of program whereby any employee who submits an idea for improvement receives recognition and some type of reward for taking the time to suggest their idea.

In an article entitled "Applied Organization Change in Industry: Structural, Technical, and Human Approaches" *(New Perspectives in Organization Research,* Wiley, 1964), Harold J. Leavitt proposes a framework for implementing system-wide change in organizations that involves three categories of consideration very similar to the people-operational-technical framework presented in this book for analyzing and solving management problems. Leavitt says that an organization can be changed systemically by changing its structure, its technology, and/or its people. Changing *structure* involves rearranging internal systems such as management information systems, lines of communication, work flow, policies, or the organization itself. Changing the organization's *technology* means altering its equipment, engineering processes, research techniques, or actual production methods. Changing the organization's *people* involves changing the selection, training, working relationships, philosophy, attitudes, or roles of the people in the organization.

The elements of structure, technology, and people are highly interdependent—a change in one is likely to affect the others. Thus an effective approach toward systemizing will take this into account. The larger the change, the more likely it will be that the change effort will have to involve all three elements to be effective. Few things are as frustrating to watch as the manager who is trying to implement a major change effort in an organization while ignoring the interdependence of these three elements.

Failure to take into account the relationships between the structure, technology, and people occurs most commonly when technological and structural changes are introduced and the effects these changes have on the human side of the organization are ignored. Another problem is created when technological changes are introduced that are incompatible with the organization's structure. The result is usually resentment and dissatisfaction among the members of the organization.

To increase the chances that changes in any of the three areas will succeed, many good managers will develop an implementation plan that addresses all three areas simultaneously. Thus, even though the problem you solve may be purely technical, and the solution is also technical, when it comes time to implement the solution, the implementation process might very well include either structural or human components or both. In the jargon of organizational psychology an approach that combines both technical and structural components is called a *technostructural* approach. One that combines people and technical is called a *sociotechnical* approach. The combination of technical and structural is called *sociostructural.*

It is important to remember that any time systemic changes are implemented the changes should be reflected and supported in policy manuals, documentation of standard operating procedures, and managment information system processes and reporting formats. Nothing will pull the rug out from under a planned change effort quicker than through the use of reporting and rewarding systems that were geared to support the old ways of doing things.

The Buck Stops with Management

As a final point in this chapter and in the book, the single most important point to remember is that no matter how good the system, or how sound the method, there is no system or technique that will guarantee success. Methods and strategies such as those presented in this book are tools to be used in a wide variety of management situations that managers are likely to encounter in the daily routine of their work. It is hoped that you will find them useful in your role as a manager. But they are only tools and should be recognized and used as such.

A carpenter should never be so frivolous as to unload his tools and expect them to build his project for him. Nor should you in your role of manager place too much blind faith in any technique or principle. For just as soon as you find something that you think will work in all situations, a new set of circumstances will arise that is likely to knock you flat on your back because you will be caught flat-footed and unprepared, having placed too much confidence in your technique.

As long as we have organizations, which will be as long as there is a demand for the goods and services organizations produce, there will be a need for managers and the functions of management. First because we will never find a substitute for the human judgment that is required to make organizations work. And foremost, because methods, techniques, and even machines don't produce organization results—managers do!

SUMMARY OF LYLES METHOD AND STRATEGIES

STEP	PROCESS STRATEGIES
DEFINE THE PROBLEM	1. Describe 2. Differentiate 3. Reconstruct 4. Separate
DEFINE OBJECTIVES	1. Seek 2. Avoid 3. Build 4. Restore
GENERATE ALTERNATIVES	1. Brainstorm 2. Copy 3. Adapt 4. Combine
DEVELOP ACTION PLANS	1. Compare 2. Force Field Analysis 3. Prioritize 4. Subjective Evaluation
TROUBLESHOOT	1. Predict 2. Exaggerate 3. Test 4. Exemplify
COMMUNICATE	1. Write 2. Verbalize 3. Promote 4. Symbolize
IMPLEMENT	1. Do It Yourself 2. Delegate 3. Phase In 4. Systemize

Index

Action plan, 148
    development of, 124
Adapt strategy, 119
Alternatives, identifying, 4
Assumptions, 30, 80
Avoid strategy, 99

Best results pyramid, 22
Brain functioning, 107
    balance, 107
    hemispheres, 109
Brainstorming, 114
Build strategy, 101

Camels are okay, 25
Combine strategy, 123
Communicating, 166
    one-way, 172
    process strategies, 172
Communication, 7, 25
Compare strategy, 134
Copy strategy, 118
Creativity, 106
    factors that hinder, 111
Critical review, 158

Data gathering, 35, 38, 81
Defining objectives, 89
    guidelines, 96
    levels for objectives, 92
    options, 93
    process strategies, 99
Delegate, 190
Describe strategy, 81
Developing action plans, 124
Differentiate strategy, 84
Do it yourself strategy, 189

Einstein, Albert, 71, 156, 166
Exaggerate strategy, 164
Exemplify strategy, 163

Facts and assumptions, 30, 80
Force field analysis, 133

Generating alternatives, 105
    process strategies, 114
Goals, 1
Group-individual-group (G.I.G.), 117

Heirarchy of purpose, 1
Heuristics, 32, 129

Implementing, 183
   guidelines, 186
   process strategies, 189

Judgment, 126

Law of Parsimony, 157
Logic, cause and effect, 76
Lyles method, 4, 10-11, 94, 103,
   124, 150, 165
   summary with process strategies,
   195

Meier, N.R.F., 46-47

Occam's Razor, 157
Osborn, Alex, 114

Phase in strategy, 191
Predict strategy, 160
Priotitize strategy, 144
Problem
   different kinds, 11
   operational, 18
   people, 13
   technical, 20
   what a problem is, 71
Problem solving, 8
   definition format, 82
   how to define, 71
   principles for defining, 73
   process strategies, 81
Promote strategy, 178

Questions
   how to ask, 35
   to define problem, 39-40

Reconstructing remote events,
   36
Reconstruct strategy, 85
Restore strategy, 103
Results, 40
Rowe, Dr. Alan, 126

Seek strategy, 99
Separate strategy, 87
Sequential solicitation, 117
Strategies
   consideration checklist, 44
   criteria for choosing, 61
   first decision, 48
   overall, 42
   second decision, 54
   selection of, 43
Subjective evaluation strategy,
   144
Symbolize strategy, 179
Systemize strategy, 192

Ten Commandments for Choosing a
   Course of Action, 130-133
Test strategy, 161
Time factors, 27
Troubleshooting, 150
   general principles, 157
   in every day management,
   156
   process strategies, 159

Verbalize strategy, 177

Wilson, M. Wayne, 182
Write strategy, 173